CULINARY AND SALAD HERBS

DESIGN FOR A HERB GARDEN
Planned by Eleanour Sinclair Rohde

CULINARY
AND SALAD HERBS

THEIR CULTIVATION AND FOOD VALUES
WITH RECIPES

by

ELEANOUR SINCLAIR ROHDE

DRAWINGS BY
HILDA M. COLEY

DOVER PUBLICATIONS, INC.
NEW YORK

This Dover edition, first published in 1972, is an unabridged republication of the work originally published by Country Life Ltd., London, England, in 1940.

International Standard Book Number: 0-486-22865-7
Library of Congress Catalog Card Number: 72-84768

Manufactured in the United States of America
Dover Publications, Inc.
180 Varick Street
New York, N.Y. 10014

TO

OUR WAR-TIME GUESTS

J. B., S. B., M. B., P. B.

WHO HAVE CONTRIBUTED SO MUCH TOWARDS
CREATING THE CHEERY ATMOSPHERE IN WHICH
THIS BOOK HAS BEEN WRITTEN

PREFATORY NOTE

Parts of this book have appeared in article form in *The Times, The Field, Gardening Illustrated,* and *My Garden,* and are reproduced in this book by kind permission of the editors of the above journals.

ELEANOUR SINCLAIR ROHDE
Cranham Lodge,
Reigate, Surrey.

CONTENTS

7

CULINARY AND SALAD HERBS

CHAPTER I

PLANNING A HERB GARDEN

I HAVE always wanted to lay out a culinary herb garden in the design of a formal Tudor rose. Rather elaborate and perhaps not very practical, because it would involve considerable labour.

In the meantime, the question I am asked by more than half the people who visit my little herb farm is whether it is possible to make a small culinary herb garden look decorative. Naturally they want a herb garden of real use. The trouble is that so many people fail to realise that the flowers and leaves of such decorative herbs as the Bergamots, Hyssop, Lavender, etc., are all edible and make a charming addition to salads. Even a small herb path in the kitchen garden can look most attractive, whereas most folk conjure up a vision of a dull little patch of Parsley, Mint, etc.

It is more amusing to make a culinary herb garden to a design, but I think the chief considerations should be an abundance of the herbs most commonly required in the kitchen and laid out in such a way that the minimum of labour is needed for upkeep. In the design given, which could well be made in a space measuring only forty by thirty feet, the eight narrow paths are edged with the herbs most commonly required—Garden Thyme, Parsley, and Chives. The two last named are tidy growers, but as Garden Thyme soon sprawls to two feet across, another possibility is to have a circle of it on the outer side of the enclosing lavender hedge. For the Lavender I would strongly advise *L. nana compacta,* and not any of the taller sorts which take up so much space. *L. nana compacta,* in my experience, comes through any winter, even that of 1939–40, without turning so much as a leaf, and never shows dead patches.   Mint is always a problem if planting to a formal design, because no member of the Mint tribe " stays put," and there is nothing for it but to grow the various mints in some corner to themselves, separating the different kinds with little hedges of Winter Savory or Dwarf Lavender.

In the solid blocks of this design are Winter Savory, Hyssop (pink and blue), Bergamot, Pot Marjoram, Tarragon, Alecost, and Balm, arranged for the best decorative effect; i.e. foliage plants such as Tarragon, Balm, etc., are put next colourful herbs, such as Hyssop and Bergamot.   It is odd how Winter Savory has rather disappeared from modern kitchen gardens, for it is invaluable.

Then there are the annuals—Chervil, Borage, Basils, Anise, Dill, Coriander, Sweet Marjoram, Summer Savory, and Nasturtiums.   I think the most satisfactory way is to grow these in clumps between the double hedge, for Dwarf Lavender does not shade sun-lovers, such as the Basils, too much.   The Lavender prevents this space looking dull till the annuals are up.

In the case of a herb path, the tall-growing plants, such as Alecost, Anchusa, Angelica, Fennel, Lovage, Orach, Rosemary, would go in clumps in the back row; those of medium height in the second row—Balm, Bergamot, Borage, Dill, Hyssop, Lavender, the upright Pennyroyal, Rampion, Rue, Sage, Savory, Chervil, Sweet Cicely, Sorrel, Tansy, Tarragon; and in front the smallest herbs, Anise, Basils, Chives, Coriander, Corn Salad, Cumin, Dandelion, Parsley, Purslane.

CHAPTER II

CULINARY HERBS

ALECOST (*Tanacetum balsamitum*)

A NATIVE of Asia introduced into these islands in very early times, possibly by the Romans, if not before. Its popular name Alecost, according to Parkinson, was given because it was used for flavouring ales. Its other popular name—Costmary—is derived from "Costus," an aromatic plant used in making perfumes in the East, and to the Virgin Mary the plant is dedicated in most western European countries. In France it is called Herbe Sainte-Marie.

Alecost is a fine upstanding plant and such a vigorous grower that it should be divided yearly. It grows about three feet high, and, unlike Tansy, to which it is closely related, the leaves are entire with finely toothed margins. The heads of small yellow flowers are borne in loose clusters in August. In this country Alecost does not set seed. It is easily increased by division either in spring or autumn, succeeds in almost any soil, but does best in a warm soil and full sun. Plant out two feet apart.

It is strange that this herb is now so seldom grown, for it is of the easiest culture and the leaves finely snipped up are a pleasant and unusual addition to salads. In France the leaves form part of stuffings for veal, etc. Costmary was formerly esteemed for its wholesome qualities and therefore used in soups, stews, etc. The dried leaves retain their aroma well and are therefore useful to add to pot-pourris.

For other uses see pages 81, 84.

ANCHUSA (*Anchusa italica*)

This herb affords one of the richest and most beautiful blues in the garden and, moreover, fairly early in the summer, for Anchusa is at its best in June. It associates well with Fennel, and when the Anchusa is past its best the foliage of the Fennel hides the rather untidy straggly growth of the faded Anchusa. Anchusa root, or rather the rind of the root, was a source of face paints, and for this was used in ancient Egypt and very commonly in this country as late as the seventeenth century. It is still used to colour ointments red.

Though a perennial, Anchusa is best treated as a biennial, sowing in May. On cold soils it is apt to die out in winter, and the young plants should be wintered in a cold frame. If the main stem is cut after flowering, smaller flowering growths are produced, which are decorative till late July. The flowers are the edible part and they look decorative in salads with pink Rose petals and Rosemary flowers.

For other uses see pages 85, 92.

ANGELICA (*Angelica archangelica*)

This is the only member of the Angelica tribe used in medicine and in the kitchen, and it is one of the few aromatic plants that is a native of northern parts of Europe, growing wild even in Lapland and Iceland. Most aromatic plants hardy in these islands are natives of the south of Europe. The plant is a biennial only in the botanical sense, being neither annual nor naturally perennial, though if the flower stems are cut down when they appear, the life of the plant can be prolonged for

ALECOST

ANGELICA

ANCHUSA

TARRAGON

several years. As a rule Angelica flowers in its third year and then dies. It is one of the handsomest herbs, with its beautiful foliage and dome-like heads of flowers which are so continually haunted by bees that it is scarcely possible to see the flowers. For decorative effect I grow Angelica as a background to Anchusa.

Angelica seed loses its germinating power extremely quickly and should be sown as soon as ripe. It seeds itself abundantly. Even in the coldest parts the seedlings come safely through the winter with no protection whatever. In the seedling stage this herb transplants easily, but after their first season the plants do not transplant so well. In the spring the seedlings should be transplanted to quite a foot apart and in the autumn transferred to their permanent quarters at least two feet apart. Angelica is extremely accommodating, but does best in moist rich soil and part shade. In any rich soil it makes very vigorous growth, the plants attaining about eight feet and about four feet through.

Formerly, almost every part of the plant was used. The root, which is white and fleshy, was used medicinally, chiefly for indigestion, the infusion being made by pouring a pint of boiling water on an ounce of the bruised root, two tablespoonfuls of this being taken three times a day. The flowering stem (cut before flowering) and the leaf stems are the parts used in making candied Angelica. The young stems of the leaves can be eaten raw like celery and an infusion of the leaves makes a pleasant aromatic drink.

To Candy Angelica

While the stalks are tender cut them in lengths of

three or four inches. Cover close and boil with very little water. Peel them and boil again till green; then dry them with a cloth. Put a pound of sugar to a pound of the stalks in an earthen pan. Let it stand covered two days and then boil the Angelica till clear and green, and put into a colander to drain. Strew as much pounded sugar over as will adhere to it and let it dry, but not become hard, in a slack oven.

Angelica and Rhubarb Jam

Rhubarb jam made with Angelica stems, using the latter in the proportion of one part to four parts Rhubarb, makes a much better flavoured confection than if Rhubarb alone is used.

Angelica Liqueur

Steep an ounce of Angelica stem finely chopped up and an ounce of peeled bitter almonds ground up in a pint of brandy for a week. Strain and add a pint of syrup made with white sugar.

For other uses see pages 81, 84.

ANISE (*Pimpinella anisum*)

A native of Greece, Crete, Asia Minor, and Egypt. One of the daintiest annuals of the Umbelliferæ. It grows about a foot high and owes its botanical name to the feathery appearance of the secondary leaflets. In this country it only ripens its seed on warm soils and in mild parts. Aniseed is not a popular flavouring in these islands, but on the Continent it is used for flavouring cakes and liqueurs and sometimes soups. The leaves of Anise have the characteristic taste (strongest in the seeds) and in moderation they are a pleasant and unusual addition to salads. They should be finely chopped up.

Sow the seed in April in light soil and in full sun. Thin to a foot apart. Anise does not transplant well, but in cold parts it may be raised under glass in March or April and transplanted, preferably each plant with a ball of soil, in mid-May. In a warm summer the seed ripens in July.

For other uses see page 84.

Asparagus Pea (*Lotus tetragonolobus*)

This is an epicure's vegetable that is particularly good served raw as a salad, masked with mayonnaise. The Asparagus Pea grows about eighteen inches high and has reddish pea-like flowers. The pods should be gathered when an inch long and boiled whole till tender. The pods are rectangular. The culture is easy. Sow the seed in April in drills two feet apart and thin to eighteen inches apart. Pods ready for use in late summer.

Balm (*Melissa officinalis*)

A native of southern Europe and naturalised in many parts of the south of England. One of the most sweet-smelling herbs, and the popular name is an abbreviation of Balsam, the choicest sweet-smelling oil of the East. Formerly Balm was highly esteemed for those suffering from nervous complaints, also from depression. It has always been a famous bee-plant. The leaves are excellent for flavouring soups, stews, etc. (allow a small handful to each half-pint), or very finely snipped up in salads. A small bunch of Balm improves claret and other cups.

Balm succeeds in almost any soil, but does best in a rich moist soil. On a rich soil it grows quite three feet high. It can be propagated by seed or division of the roots. Seed should be sown in May, the plants thinned to three inches apart, and the following season planted in their permanent quarters two feet apart. Seed is best sown in boxes of sandy soil. If propagated by division of the roots, this is best done in autumn.

Variegated Balm is most attractive, particularly in spring. It is not nearly such a vigorous grower as the type. On rich soils it reverts to type.

Balm Tea

Pour a pint of boiling water on an ounce of Balm leaves and when cool add lemon juice and sugar to taste. Or put the leaves into cold water, bring to the boil, and when cool add lemon juice, etc. In the case of most aromatic herbs the best teas are those made from the dried leaves, but balm tea is best made from the fresh leaves.

For other uses see pages 76, 79, 80, 81, 84.

BASILS

Bush Basil (*Ocymum minimum*)
Sweet Basil (*Ocymum basilicum*)

Both Bush and Sweet Basil are natives of India and are the most strongly flavoured aromatic herbs hardy enough to grow in these islands.

Bush Basil has to be treated as an annual. It makes a small bushy plant about six inches high with white flowers in whorls towards the tips of the branches. It very rarely sets seed in this country. There are several varieties, one with green, another with reddish purple leaves margined green and reddish stems, another with small leaves, a dwarf tufted form, a variety with curled leaves, and another, described as the lettuce-leaved Basil in French catalogues, is altogether of more robust growth, but has the characteristic intensely aromatic scent and flavour.

Sweet Basil grows about eighteen inches high and, like all the Basils, the leaves look as though they had been folded together along the central veins.

Basils retain their germinating power for an exceptionally long time—eight to ten years. If sown in the open, they make dwarf and late growth, but where there are no facilities for sowing under glass, it is well worth sowing in the open from mid-May onwards, for in less than two months' time they make sufficient leaf growth to be worth cutting and hanging up in bunches to dry. The Basils are so strongly flavoured that only a tiny pinch of the dried herb is needed for soup, stews, etc.

To secure good-sized plants, sow both Bush and Sweet Basils in boxes of sandy soil under glass in a temperature of fifty-five to sixty degrees in March. Thin to two inches apart. Harden off in a cold frame, and in mid-May or later in cold parts plant out eight inches apart, leaving one foot between the rows. To secure a late supply, lift some of the plants before the first frosts come and place in pots in a frost-proof greenhouse. Although the Basils are accommodating, they do best in rich soil.

Both Bush and Sweet Basils are invaluable for flavouring rich stews, soups, sausages, etc., and the fresh leaves finely snipped up and in very small quantity are a pleasant and unusual addition to salads.

For other uses see pages 77, 79, 81, 84, 104.

BERGAMOT (*Monada didyma and M. fistulosa*)

The Bergamots, especially if grown in mixed colours, are amongst the most decorative plants in the culinary herb garden. Both the flowers and the leaves are edible, and the flowers, especially those of the scarlet Bergamot, look very attractive scattered on a salad in conjunction with Borage flowers.

Bergamots do best on a light rich soil, but on very dry soils they make poor stunted growth and in a long spell of drought are apt to die out. All the tribe are easily increased by root division, and the plants should be divided at least every three years, otherwise they deteriorate. The worn-out centres of the plants should be discarded and the young outer bits planted in fresh soil. Bergamots do not ripen seed in this country. Seed is offered, however, by a few firms. The seed germinates very slowly, and I have learnt by experience that the best way is to sow it in shade. The seedlings should be pricked out in a reserve bed, also in shade, until they are large enough to transfer to their permanent positions. Bergamot flowers can be used like Rose petals in sandwiches, and so can the leaves. The latter are rather strongly flavoured.

For other uses see pages 81, 84, 85.

Borage (*Borage officinalis*)

Borage succeeds in any soil and can be sown either in March and April or in September for early flowering. Formerly the young leaves were used in salads, the tops of the plants boiled as a pot herb, and the leaves added to claret cup, etc. The flowers were also candied. The flowers are edible and very decorative in salads associated with either Rose petals or scarlet Bergamot flowers.

Caraway (*Carum carvi*)

A biennial that succeeds in any light soil. Sow in August and thin to six inches apart. Seeds used for flavouring cakes, etc.

Chervil (*Anthriscus cerefolium*)

An attractive annual growing about a foot high with lace-like leaves and umbels of diminutive white flowers. The leaves as they fade turn a pleasing shade of magenta pink. This is one of the herbs to which French cooks pin their faith, and it is excellent both in salads and for flavouring soups, stews, etc.

Chervil seed loses its germinating power very quickly and should be sown as soon as ripe. The best method is to obtain a few plants, and then they sow themselves abundantly. We have a fair-sized plot of it where it has sown itself for at least ten years. The seed ripens in July and the seedlings remain green all through the most severe winter, even such a winter as that of 1939–40. We use the thinnings in the kitchen until spring, and by that time the plants are well spaced out. Chervil is one of the very few herbs, not a sub-shrub (such as Sage,

Thyme, etc.), that can be used throughout winter.

There is a Turnip-rooted form of Chervil very rarely grown now, but which used to be commonly grown in Tudor and Stuart times. The roots are like very small Turnips, and have a peculiar aromatic, slightly nutty taste. Unlike the type, this Chervil is far from easy to grow. Seed sown in autumn germinates in spring, and sown in spring it takes a year to germinate. During its short period of growth—roughly four months—the Turnip-rooted Chervil requires no attention, beyond keeping free of weeds and watering in spells of drought. In late June the foliage fades, an indication that the roots are mature. As soon as the foliage is quite dry, the roots should be lifted and stored in sand in a dry place. The roots improve in flavour if kept for a few weeks. Stored as described, they keep perfectly through the winter. They can be cooked like Carrots, but should not be scraped.

For other uses see pages 78, 79, 80, 81, 93, 100, 102, 104.

CHIVES (*Allium schœnoprasum*)

The native habitats of this herb are wide indeed, covering the temperate and northern parts of Europe, Siberia, and North America. In these islands it is rarely found growing wild. A correspondent sent me plants and seed of some wild Chives. The grass remains in good condition long after the cultivated kind has died down. Chives are the smallest and, in the opinion of many, the best flavoured of the Onion tribe. It is a hardy perennial and the clumps increase very rapidly. I once took the trouble to split up a neglected clump measuring about fifteen inches across. It consisted of 780 bulbs, which were planted out separately. In a few months they formed clumps of about six bulbs apiece. Chives make a charming edging, especially when the flowers, which resemble those of the wild Thrift, are in bloom.

Chives can easily be increased by sowing seed, and though rarely allowed to do so, they will mature seed in the coldest parts of this country. Raising from seed (sown in May) is slower than propagating by division, the usual method. Divide the clumps yearly, either in autumn or spring, and replant about a foot apart. To secure tender " grass " the clumps should be cropped at least three times in the season, cutting each clump in turn (as required for use) fairly close to the soil. If neglected, the grass becomes tough and unfit for use. Like all the Onion tribe, Chives do best in a light soil, but to secure a continual supply of tender grass, the soil should be rich. For a very early supply put cloches over some of the roots in January.

Chives finely snipped up make an excellent flavouring for omelettes, scrambled eggs, mashed potatoes, soups, and stews, etc. For a good salad they are indispensable, though it is customary to serve the grass finely snipped up in a separate little dish, for some people dislike Onion flavouring in any form.

For other uses see pages 77, 78, 80, 84, 98, 100, 101, 104.

Coriander (*Coriandrum sativum*)

A most attractive annual and, unlike most of the aromatic spices, so hard, that when it was commonly grown in this country seed was sown in September. The seeds were harvested the following August. Coriander is a native of southern Europe and was probably introduced into this country by the Romans, if not before. It has always been a favourite spice in the East, and the Israelites must have been familiar with it, for according to Pliny, the best Coriander was that grown in Egypt. Even if the ripe seeds are not used, it is interesting to grow this culinary herb, for in Exodus xvi. 31 we are told that Manna was like Coriander seed. When green, the seed-heads are about the size of a penny and look like neat brooches. The seed when green has an intensely disagreeable taste and smell (hence the botanical name, which means " bug "). When fully ripe, the flavour is aromatic and usually much liked. The longer Coriander seeds are kept, the more fragrant they become. The leaves formerly were also used in salads and for flavouring soups, stews, etc. I am told that Indian cooks in London frequently ask for these leaves. They have a peculiar but attractive taste.

Coriander does best on a warm light soil, and it used to be grown on a commercial scale in Essex. Sow either in September or April in drills nine inches apart. The seeds are slow in germinating. Thin to four inches apart. The young leaves can be gathered as required and the seeds are ready for harvesting in August.

CORN SALAD (*Valerianella olitoria*)

The Corn Salads are given an honoured place in French catalogues and are immensely appreciated by travellers when encountered in salads abroad, yet the majority of people do not trouble to grow them in this country.   A winter as abnormal as that of 1939–40 may teach us to be more sensible, for most of the Corn Salads will survive any winter and afford good saladings when lettuces are scarce and expensive.   Gerard gives "Loblollie" as one of the popular names, and as a salading he describes Corn Salad as "among others none of the worst."   Formerly it was used both raw and cooked.   In France it is so commonly eaten during Lent that it is known also as Salade de Prêtre.

Our native Corn Salad is so called because it is common in cornfields on any soil that is not over-chalky.   Another popular name, Lambs' Lettuce, is due to the fact that it is at its best in the lambing season.   The cultivated varieties have bigger and more succulent leaves.   On the Continent the varieties chiefly grown are: (1) The round-leaved sort (Mâché rond) commonly grown by the French market gardeners round Paris.   It is a rapid and vigorous grower and very hardy.   Listed in French catalogues as Mâché à feuille ronde maraîchère parisienne. (2) Rosette Corn Salad, which has a cabbage-like appearance.   The best of these is that listed in French catalogues as verte coquille de Louviers.   (3) Etampes Corn Salad, not unlike a diminutive Savoy cabbage, which is listed in French catalogues as M. à feuille veinée or verte d'étampes.   (4) Italian Corn Salad, rather less hardy, but remains in good condition for a longer time in spring. This is listed in French catalogues as M. d'Italie à feuille de Laitue.   (5) Dutch Corn Salad, a popular variety in Holland and Germany, listed in French catalogues as M. à grosse graine.

Corn Salad does best in firm soil and should be grown in full sun.   Sow in drills six inches apart and thin the plants to six inches apart. For winter use the first sowing can be made in mid-August, and successional sowings every fortnight up to the end of September. In dry weather occasional waterings are helpful. In cold parts throw a little straw over the rows. The plants can be gathered as soon as they have made three or four leaves, using the thinnings first and then gathering the leaves.

CRESS. See MUSTARD AND CRESS.

CUMIN (*Cuminum cyminum*)

In this country we rarely use this herb nowadays for culinary purposes, but in past centuries it was commonly used, both medicinally and for flavouring cheeses, bread, etc. It is still used for these purposes on the Continent. In the East it is a flavouring ingredient in curry powder.

Cumin is a native of Egypt, and in very early times was cultivated throughout the East and in countries round the Mediterranean. In the Middle Ages Cumin was a comparatively cheap spice, but nowadays it is not easy to get the seed in this country. In appearance Cumin is an unattractive little member of the Umbelliferæ, growing barely a foot high with Fennel-like leaves and dull little magenta pink flowers. It is an annual. The seeds when green have a very unpleasant taste, but when ripe are aromatic.

In mild parts Cumin can be sown in the open, provided the soil is light and the site in full sun. Sow in mid-May and thin to four inches apart. In most parts it is best to sow in April under glass and the seedlings should be transplanted each with a good ball of earth in mid-May. The seeds are ready for harvesting in August.

DANDELION (*Taraxacum officinale*)

One of the most wholesome spring saladings, but very neglected nowadays. It would be interesting to know the real origin of the popular name by which it is called in nearly every European language. Why specially lion's teeth? And there are varieties of Dandelion with leaves scarcely dented at all. According to the section on this plant in the *Ortus Sanitatis* (1485), it is stated that this herb was much used by " Master Wilhelmus," a surgeon, who on account of its virtues compared it to " eynem lewen zan genannt zu latin Dens leonis." Another old popular name was Priest's Crown, in reference to the resemblance of the disc bearing the plumed seeds to a shaven head. Although a native of the north temperate zone, the plant is intensely sensitive to damp. The heads close directly rain falls, in fact, as a rule, just before, and always before dew-fall.

The leaves of wild Dandelions are, as a rule, very tough, but the young leaves of the cultivated form are excellent in salads. The leaves may also be cooked and served with a little grated nutmeg and a squeeze of lemon. Dandelion tea was an old-fashioned remedy for liverish people.

Dandelions succeed in almost any soil, provided it is not excessively moist. Sow the seed in April in rows a foot apart and thin the plants to a foot apart. Beyond keeping free of weeds, they need no further attention and are perennial. The blanched leaves are preferred by

CORIANDER

DILL

FENNEL

HYSSOP

some people, but they naturally have not the same health-giving qualities as the green leaves. To blanch Dandelion leaves, lift the roots and plant them in bundles of a dozen or so in a pot or box filled with soil. Cover with another pot or box, so as to exclude all light and keep in a temperature of not less than sixty degrees. Water frequently, but never over-water. Leaves will be ready in about a fortnight. Plants may be blanched in the open in spring by covering them as soon as growth shows with a thick mattress of straw, or still better by covering each plant with a flower pot, putting a stone on the hole at the bottom of each pot to exclude all light.

Dandelion Tea

Pour a pint of boiling water on to an ounce of the mature dandelion leaves, or sliced root, and infuse for a quarter of an hour. Drink at intervals during the day.

Dandelion Coffee

It is essential to use roots gathered in the autumn, for in spring the roots are almost flavourless. Wash the roots, but do not pare them. Bake them in the oven till they are a deep brown colour. When cold grind and use like coffee.

For other uses see pages 78, 81, 84, 88, 89.

DILL (*Anethum graveolens*)

This herb was commonly grown for flavouring soups, pickles, etc. It was also used medicinally, as the popular name indicates, " Dill " being derived from the old Norse

" dilla," to lull. A decoction of the seed was a homely remedy for soothing children to sleep.

Dill is a native of parts of south Europe. It is an annual and needs a light soil. Sow seed in April in drills nine inches apart and thin to nine inches apart. Dill grows very quickly and it is decorative in flower, for it grows nearly three feet high and is rather suggestive of a small Fennel, but more compact. The leaves are a good addition to salads and can be used, like Parsley, to make a fish sauce.

FENNEL (*Fœniculum officinale*), and FINOCCHIO (*F. dulce*)

Fennel (*F. officinale*) has for centuries been a popular culinary herb, but Finocchio (*F. dulce*) was only introduced in Stuart times.

F. officinale succeeds in any soil, provided the site is in full sun, and is a perennial that thrives for years. Old plants in full flower are a handsome sight, frequently covering several square feet of ground. Fennel is easily raised from seed sown in April. The leaves finely chopped can be added to salads, and with melted butter or added to a white sauce they make a pleasant change from Parsley sauce. Fennel sauce is " correct " with salmon, mackerel, or other oily fish to make them more digestible. Formerly the tender stems when a few inches high were used peeled in salads. In order to maintain a supply of leaves this Fennel should be kept cut to within a foot or so of the ground and not allowed to flower.

F. dulce (Finocchio or Florence Fennel) is one of the most popular vegetables in Italy, but in this country this delicacy is far from easy to grow. The plants grow well, but frequently fail to "bulb" at the base. Florence Fennel grows little more than two feet high, and it is essential to grow it in rich moist soil. Further, in dry spells frequent waterings are essential. When the "bulbs" swell, the soil should be drawn up to them, partly covering them. The bulb (when ready for use about the size of a hen's egg) should never be boiled, but stewed in stock and served with a cream or butter sauce.

Fennel Sauce

Remove the stems from the leaves and chop them finely. Add them either to melted butter or to a good white sauce. Either sauce should be fairly thick with the fennel.

Fennel Tea

Half a pint of boiling water poured on to a teaspoonful of crushed fennel seeds. Used as a carminative.

Fennel Seeds for Flavouring Soup

The dried seeds can be used for this purpose.

In the south of France Fennel leaves are dried and used to dip mackerel in before frying, etc. I have never heard of anyone drying Fennel in this country, but I am trying it this year.

For other uses see pages 79, 84, 93, 104.

GARLIC (*Allium sativum*)

In this country Garlic is not appreciated, but it dominates Mediterranean cookery. The most pungent member of the Onion tribe, it does best in a light very rich soil, and full sun is essential. Each bulb of Garlic consists of several cloves. Separate the cloves and put them in two inches deep and six inches apart in drills a foot apart. Beyond keeping the plants free of weeds, no further attention is needed. When the leaves turn yellow towards the end of July or early August, the bulbs can be harvested. Put them to dry in a sunny place, and when thoroughly dry tie in bunches and store in a dry frost-proof place.

Some cooks like to rub the salad bowl with a clove of Garlic, but otherwise it is rarely used.

Garlic in certain thick soups gives just the right flavouring, but it has to be used with discretion. The following is a good Italian recipe for a rich soup.

Thick Soup à l'Italienne

To four tablespoonfuls of shredded lettuce allow six tomatoes, one onion, and a few chopped olives, quarter of a clove of garlic, half-pound mushrooms, a little macaroni, three tablespoonfuls grated Parmesan cheese, one ounce butter or margarine, a teaspoonful white sugar, enough brown stock to cover, pepper, salt.

Melt the butter in the pan, add a teaspoonful of flour, and mix to a smooth paste. Add the onion (chopped up), the bit of garlic, and the tomatoes (also cut up). Add the stock, seasoning, and the chopped olives and some of the mushrooms. Simmer till soft enough to rub through a sieve. When sieved return to the saucepan, add the sugar, a little cooked macaroni, and the rest of the mushrooms (fried and cut in pieces). Stir in the Parmesan cheese and finely shredded lettuce. Serve very hot.

For other uses see page 98.

Horse-radish (*Armoracia lapathifolia*)

This herb was once famed for its medicinal properties, but is now rarely used except as a condiment. It contains a great deal of sulphur and was used for chronic rheumatism, as a plaster instead of mustard, and a homely cure for chilblains was to wrap grated fresh Horse-radish round the finger and keep in place with a piece of lint. When first used as a condiment, Horse-radish was served with fish, not meat.

Horse-radish worth eating requires a bed in full sun and rich well-cultivated soil with plenty of well-rotted manure in the bottom spit. To propagate, choose young roots barely half an inch in diameter and about a foot long, and remove any rough knots with a wooden label, but without injuring the roots. Prepare the holes for the roots by thrusting in a wooden stake into the bed semi-horizontally, i.e. so that the lower end of the hole is about four inches below the surface soil. Put each root in with the smaller end downwards and leave the other end just showing on the surface. Do not press the soil round the roots. The only further attention required is to keep the bed free of weeds and occasionally hoed. By the following autumn there should be a supply of sticks about six inches in circumference. They can be dug as required or lifted and stored. The ideal is to make a fresh bed every year, but usually a new one is made only once in three years. Make a new plantation in spring.

Horse-radish required for any of the following recipes should be grated only just before it is required, because oil of Horse-radish is very volatile and if evaporated the flavour will be poor.

Horse-radish Sauce (1)

Grate a horse-radish root very finely and to each table spoonful allow a teaspoonful of made mustard, one of white sugar, the powdered yolk of a hard-boiled egg, and a pinch of salt. Mix well and add vinegar a teaspoonful at a time until the sauce is of the right consistency. If the vinegar is added too quickly the sauce will curdle.

Horse-radish Sauce (2)

To four tablespoonfuls of grated horse-radish allow half a breakfastcupful of thick cream, one and a half tablespoonfuls vinegar, and half a teaspoonful of salt. Mix the grated horse-radish, vinegar, and salt and add lastly the cream beaten stiff.

Horse-radish Sauce (3)

To a teacupful of grated horse-radish allow an equal quantity of cream, a good pinch of salt, also of pepper, and a teaspoonful of white sugar. Mix well and then add *very* gradually a tablespoonful of vinegar.

Horse-radish Cream Sauce

To half a breakfastcupful of well-whipped cream allow three tablespoonfuls vinegar, a pinch of salt and pepper, and two tablespoonfuls grated horse-radish. When the cream is quite stiff add the vinegar *very* slowly, beating all the time. Add the salt and pepper. Lastly fold in the grated horse-radish.

Hot Horse-radish Sauce

Stew three tablespoonfuls grated horse-radish in barely half a pint of good stock. Remove from the fire and add beaten yolks of two eggs, one dessertspoonful vinegar, pepper, and salt. Stir till thick. Do not boil after egg yolks are added or sauce will curdle.

Horse-radish Relish

Into a pint of good vinegar put two ounces of grated horse-radish, half an ounce of finely chopped shallot, and a pinch of cayenne. Mix well and leave for a week. This relish should be made in November, when the roots are at their best.

Hyssop (*Hyssopus officinalis*)

This old-fashioned shrub is largely used for making hedges about three to four feet high in parts of Devon and Cornwall. In colder parts it does not grow so vigorously. The Hyssop of the Bible may possibly be *H. aristatus,* a much smaller shrub.

Hyssop is a native of southern Europe and likes a light soil and full sun. The type has blue flowers, but there are pink- and white-flowered varieties, the pink being particularly attractive. Left unclipped, it grows in a rather sprawling fashion, covering in time nearly four feet each way. It clips well, but this can only be done by sacrificing the flowers, and Hyssop honey is particularly good. On account of its strong fragrance, Hyssop was formerly used as a strewing herb, and Hyssop tea made from the fresh leaves was a homely remedy for chest troubles. Hyssop is not commonly used now as a culinary herb, and the flavour is so strong that only a few leaves finely snipped up should be added to the tablespoonful of mixed herbs for a salad.

Hyssop Tea

Pour a pint of boiling water on a quarter of an ounce of the dried leaves and infuse for fifteen minutes. Take a teacupful three times daily.

For other uses see pages 81, 84.

LAVENDER (*L. vera,* etc.)

As culinary herbs the Lavenders have to be used in very small quantities, as the flavour is so strong. The flower-heads and leaves can be used to flavour soups, stews, etc. One flower-head or four leaves to half a pint of soup is enough. We also use a leaf or so, finely snipped up, or a few flowers in the tablespoonful of chopped herbs we usually add to salads.

The hardy Lavenders commonly grown are easily increased by cuttings taken in spring or autumn. The cuttings should be of young growths about six inches long. Commercial growers prefer cuttings about three inches long, as the plants raised from cuttings of this length are less liable to Shab disease. Struck in October, the plants can be put into their permanent positions in spring, and those struck in spring should be put in their permanent positions in autumn. Deep planting is essential, i.e. the plants should be put in with barely two inches of stem left above the ground. Early autumn pruning every year is advisable, in fact, it is best done when the spikes have been gathered. Early pruning gives the plants time to make fresh growth before the cold weather sets in and is the best means of preventing dead patches. Lavender does well in most soils, but is most fragrant on chalk soils.

Lavender Toilet Vinegar

This vinegar is very aromatic and refreshing and much appreciated by the older generation of French women. Formerly it was commonly made also in this country.

Fill a quart bottle with lavender flowers, but do not put them in at all tightly. Pour in a pint of white vinegar or sufficient to cover the flowers. Leave in the sun or, failing the sun, place in a warm but not too hot corner by a stove for a fortnight. Shake every day. At the end of the fortnight empty the bottle, fill it again with flowers and filter in the vinegar already used through cotton-wool. Leave as before for a fortnight. Repeat the process a third time. By now the vinegar should be deliciously fragrant of lavender. To use, pour a little on a small piece of cotton-wool and dab on the forehead, behind the ears, etc.

Lavender Rose and Jasmine Toilet Vinegar

Dry scented rose petals, jasmine flowers, and lavender.

To four ounces dried rose petals allow one ounce each of jasmine and lavender. Put in a bottle and pour over them sufficient white vinegar to cover them. Add half-pint rose water. Leave in the sun a fortnight, or in a warm corner failing sunny weather. Strain and bottle. Use as above.

LOVAGE (*Ligusticum levisticum*)

Unlike most of the Umbelliferæ, Lovage has handsome polished foliage and in a rich soil specimens even only two or three years old are striking.

The whole plant is very aromatic, the scent of the leaves being suggestive of Celery and Parsley with an additional element of sweetness. It is strange that so pleasantly scented a herb has never attracted the attention of the poets. Lovage is a native of Mediterranean parts and the Balkans, etc., and the botanical name is said to be derived from Liguria, where it grows abundantly. It has been grown for centuries in these islands and may have been introduced by the Romans.

Lovage is accommodating and a rampant grower in any soil, but does best in rich moist soil. Like Angelica, the seeds quickly lose their power of germination and should be sown as soon as ripe. Or the plant may be propagated by root division.

The leaves of Lovage are a pleasant flavouring for soups, stews, etc., and finely snipped up they are an excellent addition to salads. In olden times the leaf stalks were blanched like Celery and the young stems candied like those of Angelica.

For other uses see pages 81, 84.

MARIGOLD (*Calendula officinale*) *

American hybridists seem to take far more interest in Marigolds than we do. I sowed a collection of the new American kinds, ranging from those with Chrysanthemum-like flowers to a miniature variety which makes tiny bushes only eight inches high with lovely lemon-yellow flowers and an outstanding kind with a wonderful scarlet sheen. All the plants except the miniature sort are two feet across with strong branching growth. But I still like best the old Pot Marigold. There is just one simple way of growing these or any annuals well, and that is to thin them early enough. It is no use waiting to thin the plants till they are a few inches high. Seed should be sown very thinly and the seedlings thinned just as soon as possible. Otherwise the plants to the last bear mute testimony to the fact that they have been left huddled miserably, and though they may grow tall, the growth is never vigorous, but floppy, and the plants have a crippled look. They should require no support at all, but stand upright in their own strength.

Marigolds in mediæval times were called just Golds, and small wonder, for in mass the old Pot Marigold looks like a sea of shimmering gold. I think it is one of the most beautiful of old-fashioned flowers. What golden modern flowers can compare with the brilliant joyous sun gold of Marigolds? They gradually acquired the name Marigolds, i.e. Golds dedicated to the Virgin Mary, for they were the flowers of her festivals.

Modern housewives make little use of Marigolds, more's the pity. A distinguished scientist who is also a doctor told me that the petals are a prophylactic against

---

*This is not the plant (*Tagetes*) called the marigold or French marigold or African marigold in the United States. It is the calendula, occasionally called the pot marigold.

cancer. Formerly Marigold petals were a common feature in salads. These petals are curiously tough, and the best way of incorporating them is to chop them up, though it is not necessary to chop them as finely as Parsley. Mixed with other chopped petals, such as Roses, Borage, Lavender, Hyssop, etc., the effect is gay and charming, and all add to the wholesomeness of the salad. Our hardy ancestors ate Marigold leaves, but they are too strong for the modern palate. At first they taste slightly sweet, but in another moment so salty as to be almost acrid.

So highly were the petals valued for their health-giving qualities that they used to be dried and stored for winter use in soups, stews, etc. Drying the petals may have been easy in leisurely days, but not now, when all our days are full of hurry. The petals have to be most carefully spread out, for if they overlap they turn an unpleasing colour. They are really best done by putting the whole flowers in layers in sand in boxes with no lids and standing these boxes in a hot cupboard. The petals turn, in about three weeks' time, a rich dark bronzy gold, but they have to be stored for keeping when perfectly dry in well-corked bottles, otherwise they lose flavour and goodness. Never dry the petals in the sun. The uses of these petals in winter are manifold. For instance, scattered on winter soups, such as lentil, or barley broth, they look very attractive. I have never tasted Marigold wine, but it used to be made in the same way as Cowslip wine.

Every possible use was made of Marigold petals medicinally. They were added to cordials, they were given in possets to cure colds. Marigold water was used for inflamed eyes, wasp and bee stings were alleviated by rubbing the affected parts with the petals, they were regarded as a remedy for warts, and they were commonly used for children's ailments of all sorts. Turner, "the Father of English Botany," observes witheringly that some women, not content with the natural colour of their hair, used the petals to turn it a golden colour, but he does not say how this was done. Conserves of the petals (made by pounding them with an equal weight of sugar to a paste) were given to those who suffered from weak hearts.

Marjoram

Pot Marjoram (*Origanum onites*)
Sweet Marjoram (*Origanum majorana*)

The most useful of the Marjorams for flavouring soups, etc., is Sweet Marjoram, for it has a unique flavour. Both Marjorams can easily be raised from seed. Pot Marjoram, being a perennial, can be increased by division, but in this country Sweet Marjoram has to be treated as a half-hardy annual.

For other uses see pages 77, 81, 84.

Mint (*Mentha spicata,* etc.)

Of the numerous varieties of Mint, *Mentha spicata* var. *viridis* is the one most commonly grown for Mint sauce. In the opinion of many epicures, however, the best Mint sauce is that made from the old Apple Mint. This handsome Mint grows four feet high, and even more in very rich soil, and, with its heads of pinkish grey flowers and attractive round leaves, it is a most decorative feature in the herb garden. Unlike Spearmint, it never suffers

LOVAGE

ASPARAGUS PEA

TREE ONION

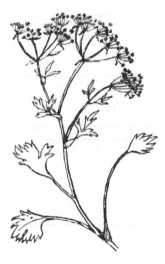

ANISE

from rust and the leaves remain in perfect condition for about six weeks longer than those of Spearmint. We use Apple Mint nearly up to Christmas. It is such a rampant grower that it is as well to keep it well away from any other plants. In fact, it needs a bed to itself, for the roots are much larger than those of any other Mint, and if left undisturbed, the ground in two seasons is solid with them.

Mentha sylvestris is invaluable, for it is fit for use when *M. spicata* is barely showing above ground, and we use *M. sylvestris* at least a month earlier than *M. spicata*. It is almost undistinguishable from *M. spicata* when young, and only goes grey or woolly later.

Mentha longifolia is grown commercially for supplying Mint early in the season, the shoots being fit to cut earlier than those of *M. viridis*. The older leaves are hairy, and consequently not easily marketable. The flavour of *M. longifolia* is inferior to that of *M. viridis*. *M. villosa nervosa,* a hybrid of *M. viridis* and *M. longifolia,* is commercially grown under glass for supplying forced Mint. The flavour of Horse Mint, *M. sylvestris,* is almost indistinguishable from that of *M. viridis,* but English cooks are so conservative that they can hardly be persuaded to use any Mint with downy leaves. *M. citrata,* sometimes called the Bergamot Mint, has a delicious scent and flavour. It is rather rare in gardens. We always dry this Mint as well as use it freshly.

Mint is commonly increased by division either in autumn or early spring. The roots should be put in horizontally two inches deep and in rows two feet apart. To secure good Mint, the bed should be given a top dressing of well-decayed manure. After some years, even given this annual feeding, a Mint bed deteriorates and a new one should be made on a fresh site. Rust is so prevalent in parts of the south that the Ministry of Agriculture advocates burning straw on all established beds of Mint annually. Choose a fine day in September or October, work the straw well in amongst the stems and a foot beyond the bed all round. The burning should be brisk and not smouldering. If properly done, the underground stems are uninjured.

The usual method of forcing Mint in private gardens is to lift the roots from October onwards at intervals of a month and plant them thickly in boxes of light soil, which are kept fairly moist in a temperature of about sixty degrees. Two- or three-year-old roots are the best to use. To secure fresh Mint during January and February the best way is to take cuttings in summer and dibble them into moist soil in boxes in a frame in a shady part. In late December or early January bring the boxes into a temperature of about sixty degrees. The sudden transference from cold to warmth and with no root disturbance makes for quick and vigorous growth.

Mint Pasty

This is an old-fashioned and most delicious north of England pasty. Take equal quantities fresh finely chopped mint, brown sugar, and currants. Mix well and pound together to a soft thick consistency. Spread between thin layers of pastry and cook till top paste is a rich golden brown.

Mint and Onion Stuffing

To three breakfastcupfuls of breadcrumbs allow nearly

one cupful finely chopped mint, a heaping tablespoonful chopped onion, two tablespoonfuls of chopped celery, fresh if obtainable, five tablespoonfuls margarine, salt and pepper. Cook the onion and celery for a few minutes in two tablespoonfuls of margarine, but do not fry. Add the mint and seasonings. Cook till steam rises well. Mix the rest of the margarine into the breadcrumbs and add the cooked ingredients.

Mint Butter

Take a large handful of mint leaves and an equal quantity of parsley. Wash well and boil slowly in as small a quantity of water as possible. Rub the pulp through a sieve. Work into four ounces of butter till the whole is perfectly smooth. Add a little cayenne pepper. (See also under Herb Butters, page 79.)

Mint Chutney

This chutney is quickly and easily made and requires no cooking, but it will not keep well longer than a fortnight. Even during that time it should be stored in very small well-corked bottles, and it is best to finish the contents of one bottle within a few days.

To a breakfastcupful of mint leaves stripped from their stems, allow a pound of sultanas or raisins, a teaspoonful of salt, four tablespoonfuls of good vinegar, and a pinch of cayenne. Put the mint leaves and the sultanas twice through the mincer, or three times if not minced finely enough. Add the other ingredients and mix thoroughly. Fill small pots, pressing down well so that no interstices are left. Cork securely.

Crystallised Mint Leaves

Wash fresh mint leaves removed from stems and dry them. Beat the white of an egg to a stiff froth and wipe over each leaf with this. Dip both sides of the leaves in granulated sugar, flavoured with oil of spearmint (allowing five or six drops of oil to a heaping tablespoonful of sugar). Pack the leaves fairly closely on a fine wire rack, cover with greaseproof paper, and dry in a very slow oven.

Mint Sauce

This sauce should not be a watery affair containing some chopped mint, but *thick* with mint. Chop the mint very finely and add brown sugar (preferably Barbados sugar) to taste—just enough to sweeten, but not more. Pour over sufficient boiling water to cover the mixture, but not a drop more. Stir well and then add good vinegar (see page 92). Mint sauce should be made several hours before being used.

Mint and Pineapple Sauce

To a breakfastcupful of well-broken-up pineapple allow an equal quantity of sugar and half a cupful of water. Simmer together for ten minutes and when cool add a tablespoonful of very finely chopped mint, five drops oil of peppermint, and green colouring.

Mint Jelly

This is a good accompaniment to cold lamb or can be used for decorating a salad.

To a pint of apple juice or white currant juice allow

a pound of sugar. Put the juice into a saucepan and add a small bunch of mint. Boil till the liquid is well flavoured with the mint. Remove the mint, add sugar, and boil till jelly sets when tested on a plate. Add green colouring and a little finely chopped mint and pour into small pots.

Mint and Gooseberry Jelly

This makes a change from red-currant jelly as an accompaniment to roast mutton.

To four pounds of green gooseberries allow two pints of water. Cook gently to a pulp. Rub through a sieve. To each pint of liquid allow a pound of sugar. Put in the preserving pan and add thirty stems of freshly gathered mint tied in muslin. Boil till the jelly sets. Pot up in small jars, as these are more convenient, for the flavour of freshly opened jars is naturally best.

Mint and Orange Jelly

This makes a decorative centre for individual salads.

To a quarter of a pint of apple or currant jelly allow a heaping tablespoonful of fresh-chopped mint and an equal quantity of grated orange rind. Break up the jelly into small pieces and roll these in the mint and orange. Serve in small cup-like lettuce leaves, adding three walnut halves to each.

Mint, Onion, Carrot, and Hamburg Parsley Salad

This is an excellent mixture. Pound finely a sliced small onion with four ounces fresh mint leaves. Add two heaping tablespoonfuls of raw carrot and the same of Hamburg parsley root. Mix well and add lemon juice, salt, and pepper. If preferred, the onion can be grated.

Mint-flavoured Carrots

Cut four carrots in slices about a quarter-inch thick. Cook for fifteen minutes, drain, and then put the carrots into a mixture of half a breakfastcupful of butter or margarine, same quantity of sugar, and a heaping tablespoonful of finely chopped mint leaves. Cook gently till the carrots are soft. Add cooked peas and salt and pepper. Serve very hot.

Mint and Fruit Punch

To a quarter of a pint of any soft fruit juice (currants, raspberries, strawberries) allow the juice of one orange, two handfuls of fresh mint, and a little castor sugar.

Bruise the mint thoroughly, put it in a jug, and pour on to it a quart of boiling water. Stir well and leave for half an hour. Strain, add the other ingredients. Serve cold in individual glasses with a sprig of mint floating on each.

Mint Syrup. (This makes a pleasant summer drink, diluted to taste with water.)

To half a breakfastcupful of water allow an equal quantity of sugar, half the quantity of lemon juice, and two heaping tablespoonfuls of mint. Boil sugar, mint, and water together for five to ten minutes. When cool add the lemon juice, also green colouring. Strain through clean muslin.

Mint Cordial

Pick the leaves off a large bunch of mint. Wash them and bruise them thoroughly in a bowl. Add the juice of two large lemons and leave for quite two hours. Boil a breakfastcupful of sugar with a pint of water for fifteen minutes and pour into the bowl containing the lemon juice and mint. Strain, add the juice of two sweet oranges, half a pint of pineapple juice, and dilute with a little water to taste. Serve in slender glasses, each half-filled with crushed ice and adorned with a spray of mint.

Mint Lemonade

Pound a handful of fresh mint leaves with five teaspoonfuls of sugar. Peel three lemons finely and pound the rind with the flesh and mint syrup. Add a pint of water, stir well, and leave for an hour. Strain through fine muslin, serve with bits of lemon peel, and a sprig of mint in each glass.

Mint Julep

To a breakfastcupful of fresh lemon juice allow half a cupful of water, a bunch of mint leaves (as much as the lemon and water will hold), and one and a half cupfuls of sugar. Mix these ingredients and leave for half an hour. Pour over a large piece of ice and add three pints of ginger ale. Serve in glasses.

For other uses see pages 75, 78, 79, 80, 81, 84, 101.

MUSTARD (*Sinapis nigra*)

There are two varieties of the common Mustard—

Black Mustard and White Mustard. The leaves of the former are much more "mustardy" than those of the latter, and most people prefer White Mustard leaves for salading. The leaves of all other vegetables, even when gathered young, are at any rate partially developed, but Mustard is gathered usually before the true leaves have been formed. When Mustard was first used as a condiment is uncertain, but it is a well-known fact that the Romans were great mustard eaters. They made mustard sauce by pounding the seeds with wine. In olden times in this country mustard seed was pounded and made into balls with vinegar or honey and cinnamon, kept thus, and then dissolved in more vinegar when required for use. The best mustard in Elizabethan times was that made at Tewkesbury, and in *Henry IV* there is a reference to this. A certain Mr. Clements of Durham is always credited with having invented the modern method of preparing mustard flour towards the close of the eighteenth century, and for many years the best mustard was sold as " Durham Mustard." Mustard for making the condiment on a commercial scale is grown chiefly in Lincolnshire and Yorkshire.

As a salading Mustard, like Cress, is most appreciated in winter and very early spring. In a greenhouse with a temperature of fifty degrees it can easily be grown. Seed should be sown evenly on fine soil, pressed firm either in boxes or pans. Press the seed into the soil, but do not cover it. When watering has to be done, never give water straight from the main, but water that has stood in the greenhouse for twelve hours. Both Mustard and Cress can also be easily grown on a sunny window sill, and where soil is lacking, even on flannel.

An economical way where a box of soil is used is to scrape off the remains of the stalks after cutting, sprinkle with fresh soil, and resow. Some people sow a little fresh salading every day like this, using several boxes. Mustard seed germinates more quickly than that of Cress, and therefore it is customary to sow Cress three days before the Mustard with which it is to be eaten. Out of doors Mustard and Cress can be sown for succession from March to October, either broadcast or in drills. Mustard takes about ten days to reach the stage at which it is usually cut, and Cress takes quite a fortnight.

Flavoured Mustards

The most expensive flavoured mustards are those imported from abroad. Dijon was formerly famous for the mustards made there, these mustards being flavoured with Tarragon, Capers, Anchovies, etc. Some people like a very mild mustard, and this is easily made by mixing mustard flour of a good brand with cream, or even top milk, a pinch of salt, and just two or three drops of tarragon vinegar. Mustard can be flavoured with parsley, tarragon, shallot, chives, chervil, etc., by making a very thin mustard and in sufficient quantity to leave the required herb steeping in it, using five teaspoonfuls of the herb to each half-pint of mustard. Shallot has to be bruised. Leave the herbs steeping for a week and then strain off. Home-flavoured mustards should be kept in well-corked bottles.

Chinese Mustard

Of all the large-leaved Mustards, this is, I think, the

best. A few years ago I developed a sudden enthusiasm for the Mustard tribe and grew a number of them, most of them with leaves larger than the largest Spinach leaves, and some of them decoratively frilled and waved. But Chinese Mustard is one of the best for salads, and it can be cooked like Spinach. It flourishes in almost any soil. Like the other Mustards, it can be sown for succession up to August. Thin to six inches apart.

For other uses see page 85.

Orach (*Atriplex hortensis*)

There are three well-known varieties of Garden Orach, or Mountain Spinach—green, white, and red. The type is a native of Tartary and was commonly cultivated in these islands in Tudor times. It was used both raw in salads and cooked, but after the introduction of Spinach, Orach rapidly lost its popularity. In French catalogues several varieties of Orach are listed, the white being the most esteemed. The red Orach is the most attractive in appearance with its blood-red five-feet-high stems and leaves of the same colour. It is especially attractive in seed, for the seeds are also blood-red. The young leaves are decorative in salads. The older leaves are cooked like Spinach, i.e. in their own juice.

For other uses see page 85.

Parsley (*Carum petroselinum*, syn. *Petroselinum hortense*)

The original habitat of Parsley is uncertain, but is now believed to be Sardinia. The date of its introduction into this country is unknown. The Italian or plain-leaved Parsley is seldom grown now, the most popular being the moss-curled kinds, but the plain leaved stands the winter best, as the leaves do not hold the damp. Parsley can be sown for succession from spring to August, but the chief sowings should be made in early April and again in August to stand the winter. Both the April- and August-sown plants come through the following winter, but the April-sown runs to seed very early in the season. It is therefore always advisable to make the two sowings. Few people thin Parsley either early enough or sufficiently far apart. One of the large kinds will fill a square foot of ground easily, and grown thus as an edging herb is very striking. Rich but well-drained soil secures the best results. Sow the seed in drills fifteen inches apart and thin like Turnips, i.e. at no stage allow the leaf of one plant to touch a leaf of its neighbour.

Most people associate Parsley with the superstition that the seed is so slow in germinating because it goes seven times and back to the Devil. There are still old-fashioned gardeners who decline to transplant Parsley on the score that it brings bad luck, and there is a French proverb, " Repiquer le persil repiquer sa femme." The double-curled Parsley once so popular in cottage gardens is said to have originated by sowing on Good Friday. I can vouch for the truth of the following: An artist in the west of Ireland who was staying with cottage folk could not sleep for fleas. A peasant told her that if she put Parsley leaves under the bed she would sleep in peace. She did and was not molested any more. The odd thing is that in Chinese one name for Parsley signifies " kill flea." I wish some scientific-minded person would explain or, anyhow, test seriously whether there is anything in the belief that if Parsley is planted round the Onion bed it keeps away the Onion fly. I know various people who say that in their experience this is true.

Parsley Basket

In my childhood cottagers used to make parsley baskets, and very pretty they were. These baskets were made by lining a wire basket with moss and filling it with good soil, and then about a dozen parsley roots were pushed in at the top, bottom, and sides and the soil made very firm. The baskets were hung in the porch or any sunny window, and well-tended specimens looked like balls of foliage. The more the leaves were picked, the more thickly the plants grew, and they were kept well moistened.

To chop Parsley Finely

To chop Parsley finely without a parsley cutter requires a little skill. Never attempt to chop Parsley wet. After washing, dry it in a cloth, and if fine sharp scissors are not available, collect the Parsley between the thumb and first finger of left hand, press well together, and cut with a sharp knife. Gather up the Parsley again and again cut. Continue till the Parsley is chopped finely enough. A little practice soon enables anyone to do this quite quickly.

Parsley Tea

This was a noted old-fashioned cure for rheumatism. To make it, put a good handful of parsley, including the stems, into a pint of cold water. Bring slowly to the boil and simmer gently for half an hour. Drink half a pint twice a day.

Parsley-root Tea

Half a pound of parsley roots to a pint of water. Bruise the roots thoroughly and then boil them gently in the water. Strain. Take a wineglassful night and morning. (This was formerly a homely remedy for kidney troubles.)

To fry Parsley

Parsley to be fried should be freshly picked, and as it shrinks considerably in frying, at least four times the bulk required should be used. Wash thoroughly and remove all stalks. Dry thoroughly, put into a frying basket, and lower very gently into the fat. The fat should *not* be smoking hot. Usually fried Parsley is an accompaniment to a fried food, so it is best to use the fat for this dish and then leave the fat for a few minutes till the temperature drops a little. Parsley makes fat froth considerably, and consequently it is necessary to lower the frying basket with the parsley very gently into the fat. The parsley is ready when the sizzling stops, and this takes about a minute. Drain thoroughly first over the fat and then on paper. Season the parsley and serve it very hot. The important points to bear in mind are, dry the parsley very thoroughly, do not use fat that is too hot, do not over-fry parsley.

Parsley New Potatoes

New potatoes sprinkled with parsley are good, but the following is a better method:

BERGAMOT

SWEET BASIL

SWEET CICELY

ORACH

To two pounds of quite small new potatoes allow nearly a breakfastcupful of finely chopped parsley, the juice of half a lemon, and a little melted butter (margarine in war-times). Mix the lemon juice and melted butter thoroughly. Roll the hot potatoes in this and then in the parsley. Serve at once.

Parsley Jelly

This is an excellent accompaniment to cold meat, especially cold chicken. It can also be used as a sandwich filling. To make it, fill a preserving pan with fresh parsley leaves and scarcely cover with cold water. Bring to the boil and simmer gently for half an hour. Add the juice of a large lemon to every pint of liquid and put in also the lemon rinds. Strain, measure, and to every pint of juice allow a pound of lump sugar. Return to pan and boil until the jelly sets when tested on a plate. Pour into small jars and cover when cold.

To dry Parsley

Drying Parsley well is difficult. The method used in drying other herbs is not usually very successful. After washing the leaves and then dipping them in boiling water, it is best to put them in a very hot oven for exactly one minute. The leaves should not be at all scorched, but brittle. Bottle immediately and cork securely. With an Aga cooker the easiest way is not to wash the parsley, but to lay the sprays as soon as gathered on the *lid* of the boiling side. The sprays dry perfectly and remain a rich green. The method of dipping the sprays in boiling water to which a pinch of bicarbonate of soda has been added keeps the colour, but it is unwholesome, just as unwholesome as keeping boiled greens a bright colour by the same deplorable method.

HAMBURG PARSLEY (*Carum petroselinum fusiformis*)

This variety of Parsley was appreciated at its proper value in Victorian times, but for some unaccountable reason is rarely grown now. It was introduced by Philip Miller in 1727. It is one of the most valuable of winter saladings, for the roots, which in good ground grow to about the size of large Carrots, are delicious raw, and they grate to the consistency of milled nuts. This Parsley is so hardy that all through the severe winter of 1939 the green tops of ours on heavy soil remained green and the roots in perfect condition till the end of February. The tops may be used like common Parsley for flavouring, but are unsuitable for garnishing, for they grow quite eighteen inches high and are quite plain. The roots have a white skin and should not be peeled before using. They make an excellent salad grated raw and masked with mayonnaise or mixed with other salad ingredients. Like all root vegetables, they should be grated only just before use, as they turn colour.

PENNYROYAL (*Mentha pulegium*)

This is such a powerfully flavoured herb that it has to be used with discretion for culinary purposes. It was the chief flavouring ingredient in a pudding called Pudding Grass, of the type for which a recipe is given on page 78. But nowadays, in the making of such a pudding, Pennyroyal can be used only in small quantities, a pinch being sufficient. There are two varieties of Pennyroyal, the creeping and the rare upright form. The latter is not only the most attractive in appearance, especially in flower in late August, but it is the most useful to grow in the culinary herb garden because it is easily collected and tied in bundles to dry, whereas the creeping form is more trouble. To harvest for drying, the stems should be cut just before the plants flower.

Both forms of Pennyroyal are easily increased by division, either in autumn or spring. Autumn is preferable in most parts because, especially on cold soils, the plant frequently shows no growth above soil till late May. It is then the hot weather begins, which is quite unsuitable for planting out a moisture-loving plant.

Pennyroyal Eggs

Make buttered eggs in the usual way and put in, before they are quite cooked, finely chopped pennyroyal. A pinch of Madras curry powder may be added also.

PURSLANE (*Portulaca oleracea*);
GOLDEN PURSLANE (*P. sativa*)

The original habitat of this herb is unknown, but it has been cultivated from time immemorial and was highly valued for its medicinal properties, as an anti-magic herb, and for salads and culinary purposes. The origin of the popular name is also unknown. In the *Grete Herball* (1516) it is called " Procelayne."

Unlike most leaves used in salads, the leaves of the

Purslanes are thick and fleshy, and the golden-leaved kind is most decorative. The Purslanes revel in a sandy soil. Sow for succession from mid-May onwards and then thin the plants to six inches apart. Though they like a sandy soil, the Purslanes are appreciative of plenty of moisture during spells of drought. Kept well cut, the plants produce fresh leaves; but allowed to flower, the leaves become worthless for salads. The golden kind is rather less hardy than the green.

In salads Purslane leaves, stripped from their stalks (the stalks are tough), are very palatable, and the leaves, together with Sorrel, are used to make the French soup "bonne femme." The leaves make attractive and unusual sandwiches if put in layers between thin slices of brown bread and butter. Formerly the stalks were pickled by boiling them in wine and then covering the cooked stalks with vinegar and adding sugar to taste.

Seventeenth- and eighteenth-century cookery books give many Purslane recipes, including Purslane soup. Giles Rose, who was one of the master cooks to Charles II, served " Sallets of lettice and Purslan " thus: " Take of the newest Purslan, pick and wash it very well, swing it out and land it round of the Plate and Lettuce round about it, garnish the brims with Chervil and Flowers of divers colours, very small." This must have been an uncommonly pretty salad—the reddish golden stems and fleshy leaves of the Purslane contrasting with the vivid green of the Lettuce leaves and the whole surrounded with lace-like Chervil and mixed edible flowers, probably Borage, Marigolds, Rosemary, Anchusa, Rose petals, etc.

I am always meaning to try the Purslane soup recipe

given by Vincent la Chapelle who was cook to the
Prince of Orange in 1744. "Boil the Purslane in pea
soup with a little onion, when your Purslane is boiled
enough soak some crusts in the broth, garnish them
with Purslane, pour over the broth and serve it up hot."

Perhaps I should add that in those days "Pea soup"
was made from the died seeds of Chick Peas. It appar-
ently never occurred to anyone to eat green Peas. The
famous Roncesvalles Pea listed in nurserymen's catalogues as late as Victorian times was grown originally,
both in this country and France, for the sake of the
seeds, which were stored for winter use. It was
Louis XIV who started the fashion for eating Peas green,
and the diarists of the period state that he was frequently
ill, owing to the enormous quantities of this delicacy
that he consumed.

RADISH (*Raphanus sativus*)

The original habitat of this species of Radish is unknown, but it may have descended from *R. raphani-
strum*, a native of Mediterranean parts. The popular
English name is from the Saxon "reod" (ruddy), and
refers to the red colour of the roots. Radishes are
amongst the oldest cultivated vegetables. Before the
Christian era they were well known in ancient Egypt.
The Romans may have introduced them into this
country, though quite possibly they may have been
known before.

In my childhood, Radishes, like Watercress, were regarded as cottagers' saladings, but fashion is as capricious
in the vegetable world as elsewhere. For Radishes have

" riz " and are no longer tolerated as merely decorative features in a salad. The odd thing is that very few people (anyhow of my acquaintance) have ever eaten the best part, i.e. the seed pods. The flavour is better than that of Radishes and less hot, and thin brown bread-and-butter sandwiches, with a layer of seed pods, are first-rate. Incidentally, if margarine has perforce to be used, they conceal the taste of it. Radish seed pods can also be pickled.

It is not commonly realised that Radishes fall into two distinct categories: (1) those that are best sown in spring and summer; and (2) winter Radishes. If winter Radishes are sown earlier than July, they are almost certain to run to seed. Radishes for spring sowing are mostly rather small, and they can be grown to perfection only in light rich soil. If slowly grown, they are invariably tough and uneatable. Old-fashioned gardeners used to mix Radish seed with seed of early Carrots. The Radishes matured quickly and were drawn before the Carrots needed all the space. They also used to sow Radishes on top of first-early Potatoes. The Radishes helped to protect the Potatoes and were drawn long before the shaws made much growth.

One of the commonest mistakes with Radishes is to sow the seed too deeply. It is for this reason that many experienced gardeners prefer broadcast sowing and lightly beating the surface afterwards with a spade. If sown in rows, the seeds should be only just covered and then made firm. As soon as the seedlings appear above ground, they should be thinned. Delay involves slower growth and inferior produce. Winter Radishes that make big roots have to be thinned to six inches apart.

Amongst winter Radishes the pick are Black Spanish, Japanese Colossal, and Japanese Yard Long. All these make large roots, the round Black Spanish being the size of largish Potatoes. In spite of their size, these Radishes are tender and are a very good addition to a winter salad grated raw. There are both round and long Black Spanish, the former being the best. Japanese Colossal makes very large roots, and Japanese Yard Long makes roots about two feet long and with a diameter of about three inches. All these Radishes can be stored like Potatoes, but, in common with most root vegetables, the flavour of the freshly lifted roots is best.

Radishes in Cold Frames for use in January

Radishes are most appreciated in January and very early spring. To secure them as soon after Christmas as possible, sow them the first or second week in October. Sow in a frame of old potting soil and keep the lights closed till germination takes place, and then remove the lights entirely. Protection will only be necessary in case of frost. For a supply in January and February sowings must be made on a hotbed three feet deep and a foot larger than the frame to be put on it. When the temperature remains below seventy degrees, cover the hotbed with four inches of finely sifted soil. Sow the seed either broadcast or in rows, sowing very thinly and evenly, press firm and just cover with fine soil. Until germination has taken place, keep the frames covered with mats, but as soon as this has taken place, remove immediately. Even a few hours' delay results in drawn plants. On mild days tilt the lights a little, but close early. Should watering be necessary, give lukewarm water through a fine rose. Sown at this season, the crop takes about seven weeks to mature.

Many people find Radishes too hard, but they can be reduced to fairy-like flakes put through a mincer and look most attractive in this form. Mixed with grated Carrot and with the addition of mayonnaise sauce, they make a delicious salad when greenstuff is scarce. Small white Radish can be used as a substitute for early Turnips in stews, etc., or they can be boiled and served with melted butter.

RAMPION (*Campanula rapunculus*)

When in flower, there is a fairy-like quality about this once-popular salad herb. It is not unlike a Harebell on slender stems two feet high. Rampion figures in fairy lore rather conspicuously. The heroine Rapunzel in one of Grimm's fairy tales is called after this herb, and the tale is woven round the theft of Rampion roots from a magician's garden. According to a Calabrian legend, a village maid who gathered a root of this plant in a field found that the hole left led down to a palace in the depth of the earth.

Rampion, a hardy biennial, is a native of parts of south Europe and a doubtful native in this country, for it was formerly so commonly grown as a salad and pot herb that where it now grows wild it may have naturalised itself. The root resembles a diminutive Turnip, and hence the botanical specific name, "rapunculus." The roots can be eaten either sliced raw in salads or cooked. They have a rather sweet flavour. The young leaves can be eaten raw.

Sow the seed in May, June, or July in drills six inches apart, preferably in rich soil and part shade. Thin plants to four inches apart. The roots are ready for use from November onwards, and they can be stored like Carrots, but are better fresh.

To cook Rampion

Boil or steam the roots till they are tender. They take about half an hour. Serve with a good white sauce.

ROSEMARY (*Rosmarinus officinalis*)

Like Lavender, this herb has too powerful a flavour to be used much for culinary purposes. A leaf or two is enough to flavour half a pint of soup or stew, but the flowers are a very pleasant addition to salads.

Rosemary does well in the open only in very mild parts. It is best grown against a sunny wall or fence, and in such a position flowers very early. Slips taken with a heel can be struck in very sandy soil in September. In cold parts they must be struck in a cold frame. Or raise from seed sown in May, but Rosemary is very slow-growing compared to the smaller aromatic shrubs, such as Sage, Rue, Southernwood, and Winter Savory.

Rosemary Tea

Pour a pint of boiling water on a handful of the leaves and flowers. Take half a pint daily for a cold.

Rosemary Sugar

Pound young rosemary leaves with three times their weight in sugar.

Rosemary Hair Wash

Two ounces rosemary, two ounces southernwood, and half an ounce of camphor. Put all the ingredients in a jug and pour on a pint of boiling water. Leave for one hour. Strain and bottle. Apply to the scalp daily.

RUE (*Ruta graveolens*)

Owing to its bitterness, Rue is little used for culinary purposes. We find just as much as will cover a three-penny bit (not the new coin, but the old) is quite enough snipped up to add to the tablespoonful of mixed herbs for a salad. Rue tea was formerly a popular remedy for indigestion.

Rue is easily raised from seed sown in spring, or strike cuttings in spring in very sandy soil. Rue grows quickly, and to keep the bushes shapely they should be clipped in spring, cutting back to young growths. Variegated Rue is a most attractive sub-shrub, but in good soil reverts to type.

Rue Tea (for Indigestion)

To a handful of rue leaves allow a quart of boiling water. Put the rue in a jug and pour on the boiling water. Cover and leave for twenty-four hours. Dose, a wineglassful daily.

SAGE (*Salvia officinalis*)

Few cooks regard the flowering variety of this Sage with favour, which is a pity, for the flowers are a decorative and aromatic addition to salads. The flowering form of the red variety is not so common as the non-flowering form. It is very attractive, for the reddish foliage shows off the Lavender-blue flowers to perfection. I have the blue-, pink-, and white-flowering varieties of the green Sage, and very delightful they are in mass, for by the end of May, no matter how cold the season, they are always sheeted with blossom. And how the bees love the flowers! Sage sports freely, and apart from the varieties mentioned, there are broad- and narrow-leaved kinds and variegated sports of both the green and red Sage. Formerly, the narrow-leaved form was regarded as better for both culinary and medicinal purposes.

In common with most herbs that are natives of Mediterranean parts, Sage does best in a light soil. In cold parts even the flowering varieties rarely flower well, if at all. Sage deteriorates quickly and should be raised from cuttings at least every four years. Take cuttings with a heel and strike in May in very sandy soil in open. Sage is also easily raised from seed, but cannot be relied upon to come true to type. Seed should be sown in May.

Sage Tea

(1) To a handful of the leaves allow a pint of boiling water. Put the leaves in a jug and pour on the water. The infusion is ready when cool enough to drink. Dose, half a pint daily.

(2) To a handful of the leaves allow the juice and rind of one lemon and an ounce of sugar. Add a pint of boiling water. Make in the same way as above.

Sage and Onion Sauce (to serve with Roast Duck, etc.)

To every ounce of onion allow half an ounce of sage leaves, a quarter of an ounce of freshly grated lemon peel, a very little minced shallot, a teaspoonful of vinegar, a walnut of butter or margarine, a teaspoonful of flour, seasoning, and half a pint of brown gravy or stock. Put the butter or margarine in a pan, sprinkle in the flour, and cook for three minutes or so, stirring till it is a smooth paste. Mince the onion and sage finely. Put them and the rest of the ingredients into the pan. Cover closely and simmer for half an hour.

The above recipe with the addition of bread can be used to make sage-and-onion stuffing.

Sage Jelly

Make in the same way as Parsley Jelly (see page 56).

SAVORY

SUMMER SAVORY (*Satureia hortensis*)

An annual raised from seed sown in April in drills a foot apart. Thin the plants to six inches apart. Does best in a rich light soil, but is very accommodating. Seed germinates very slowly. The tops can be used any time, and for harvesting the rows should be pulled up in August when in flower.

The flavour of Summer Savory is rather like that of Marjoram. In France it is regarded as the correct accompaniment to Broad Beans. Serve the Beans (after slipping off their hard coverings) with melted butter or margarine poured over them, and strewn with finely chopped Summer Savory. Like Winter Savory, this herb is excellent for flavouring stuffing for veal, turkey, sausages, etc.

It was formerly regarded, like Winter Savory, as a specific for bee stings. A leaf rubbed on the affected part gives instant relief.

For other uses see pages 75, 77, 78, 79, 80, 81, 84, 86, 93, 98, 100, 104.

WINTER SAVORY (*Satureia montana*)

Both Summer and Winter Savory were more appreciated than they are now when East Indian spices were a luxury the rich alone could afford. For the Savories are the most strongly flavoured of the hardy aromatic herbs, and second only to the Basils and Sweet Marjoram, which are half-hardy.

Winter Savory, being evergreen, is useful in winter. It succeeds in most soils, but in cold parts does best in poor, very well-drained soil, for in rich soil it makes too much sappy growth to stand the winter. Winter Savory can be raised from seed (but seed germinates very slowly) and is easily propagated also by striking cuttings of side-shoots in late spring or early summer in a cold frame. The frame must be kept closed till the cuttings have rooted (about five weeks). Raised from seed, the plants flower their second season. Winter Savory remains in good condition for about five years, but it is advisable to raise fresh stock every four years, for in a severe winter the older plants suffer badly. This herb is particularly useful for flavouring stuffings for veal and turkey. It is excellent in Lentil soup. Like Summer Savory, a leaf rubbed on a bee sting gives immediate relief.

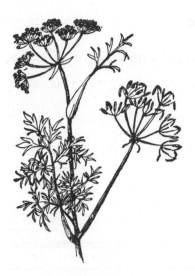

CARAWAY

CHERVIL

PURSLANE

CHIVES

Sweet Cicely (*Myrrhis odorata*)

Old plants of Sweet Cicely are extremely decorative with their huge fern-like leaves, and when about five feet high the plants are amongst the most impressive in the herb garden. Sweet Cicely is extremely slow-growing. In fact, as both Lawson and Gerard emphasised three centuries ago, they are amongst the slowest-growing perennials. Sweet Cicely is a native plant and formerly was highly appreciated for its health-giving qualities, the leaves and roots being used in salads, the leaves raw, and the roots boiled and sliced. The leaves are exquisitely soft, almost silky to the touch, and their flavour is anise-like and they taste as though they had been sprinkled with white sugar.

Sweet Cicely seeds itself liberally. The seeds quickly lose their germinating power, and if collected they should be sown immediately. They often do not germinate till the following spring. Thin the plants to three inches or so apart during their first season, and the following autumn plant out in their permanent positions. Sweet Cicely makes enormous roots, reaching down quite two feet. Parkinson, three hundred years ago, accurately described their flavour as " sweet pleasant and spicie hot, delightfull unto many." The seeds also are spicy, but I should not describe them as pleasant. The leaves snipped up are a good addition to salads, and are also useful for flavouring stews, etc.

For other uses see pages 81, 84.

Sorrel (*Rumex scutatus and R. acetosa*)

The Garden Sorrel (*R. scutatus*) is a native of southern

parts of France, also of large parts of Italy, Switzerland, and Germany. It has retained its popularity in the countries of which it is a native, and is used in soups, stews, etc. *R. acetosa,* a native of these islands, is decidedly more acid, and lost its popularity for culinary purposes after the cultivation of French Sorrel became more common. Formerly, however, it was used chiefly to make a sauce with cold meat, and hence the popular name Green Sauce. It was also used instead of Apple Sauce with roast pork or goose. *R. acetosa* is so intensely acid that, if used as a vegetable and not merely as a sauce, many people prefer to boil it in two waters, the first time for three or four minutes to get rid of the excess acid. Some people like to use Chopped Sorrel in omelets. Also a leaf or so in soups.

Both the Sorrels mentioned are perennials and can be either raised from seed or propagated by division of the roots. *R. acetosa* does best in a damp soil and *R. scutatus* in a dry warm soil. French catalogues list varieties of *R. scutatus,* one of the best being Oseille de Belleville.

Herb Patience (*R. alpinus*), also a perennial, is a doubtful native. It attains about six feet when in flower. The leaves are not very palatable, and I grow it only for the sake of its pretty name. It is a native of Italy, and one of its popular names, Monks' Rhubarb, refers to the fact that it was formerly grown in monastery gardens for its medicinal properties.

Sorrel Sauce for Roast Duck

Stew sufficient sorrel leaves in their own liquor to make a quarter of a pint of juice. Mix with an equal quantity of gravy. Rub six or so gooseberries through a sieve and add them with a little sugar. Serve very hot.

TANSY (*Tanacetum vulgare*)

Formerly this was one of the commonest culinary herbs, and even in my childhood it was grown in almost every cottage garden, especially the charming double-curled variety, now almost lost to cultivation. But though Tansy was formerly so commonly used, especially in the Tansy cakes made for the Easter festival, it has to be used nowadays in very small quantities. We have not the liking for such pungent flavouring as our ancestors, and only a portion of a leaf, about a quarter of an inch long and as much broad, finely chopped up, is enough for a large salad. I do not think we should appreciate Tansy cakes nowadays.

Tansy is a rampant grower, and should never be put near any choice plants, for the roots soon fill solidly several square feet of ground. The old curled Tansy is very attractive, especially in spring, when only about six inches high.

TARRAGON (*Artemisia dracunculus*)

The two Tarragons commonly cultivated in this country are *A. dracunculus* var. *sativa,* usually though inaccurately called French Tarragon (it is a native of Central Asia) and Russian Tarragon, *A. Redowskii,* a native of Siberia.

The Tarragons do best in a sandy soil and a sheltered part. They are propagated by division of the roots in spring or autumn or by cuttings taken with a heel of the side growths that have not flowered. Strike the cuttings in August in a cold frame kept closed till they have rooted (about six weeks). Most herbs required for drying are gathered just before they show flower buds, but Tarragon is harvested in August.

Tarragon Vinegar (see page 81).

For other uses see pages 77, 78, 79, 80, 81, 84, 92, 93, 95, 97, 101.

TREE ONION

This is a useful form of the common Onion to grow for salads, for the tiny onions produced at the tips of the stems are just the right size when a little Onion flavouring is required for a salad. It is extravagant to cut a whole Onion for the purpose. The Tree Onion produces bulbs at the base and at the tips of the leaves very small bulbs. It can be increased either by division of the root bulbs or by planting out the small bulbs in autumn. If left ungathered, these small bulbs bend over and plant themselves round the parent plant.

WELSH ONION (*Allium fistulosum*)

This member of the Onion tribe is as valuable in midwinter as Chives during spring and summer. During the last abnormal winter we were gathering the grass literally through the snow. The foliage was abundant all through the worst weeks. This Onion is a native of Siberia, and presumably owes its popular name to the fact that at one time it was so commonly grown in Welsh cottage gardens. It is a perennial that forms no bulbs, the foliage being used for flavouring salads, soups, etc. It is best raised annually from seed sown in drills a foot apart in March and April. Established plants can be divided every three or four years.

CHAPTER III
THE DRYING OF HERBS

I THINK the commonest mistake amateurs make in drying herbs is to attempt drying on far too large a scale at once. The easiest way is to dry just one bunch of herbs each day, and it is surprising what a valuable store can thus be accumulated for the winter. If for household use, there is, as a rule, no need to dry the herbs separately. The Basils are perhaps an exception, for they are so strongly flavoured that it is best to dry them separately.

Herbs to be dried are generally best gathered before they come into flower, for the flavour is then at its strongest. The ideal time is early morning after the dew dries off them and before the sun is at its hottest. It is always a mistake to dry either in the sun or a strong wind, for the essential oils the leaves contain are quickly dispersed under such conditions. Tie the herbs in small loose bunches. Large bunches dry slowly, for the air cannot circulate freely amongst the leaves, and consequently the flavour will be impaired. A dry warm room with a slight current of air blowing through is ideal. Farmers' wives in my childhood used to hang up bunches of herbs to the kitchen ceiling, and though the bunches may have collected a little dust, it was an ideal place to hang them, for hot air rises. In those days, when home-made sausages were flavoured with Sage, etc., really well-dried herbs made all the difference, and housewives took pride in the excellence of their flavourings. Sometimes a dry shed is the most suitable place in which to dry them, and in this case the simplest way is to run strings across about nine feet above the ground-level and tie the bunches of herbs to them. Another practical method is to run strings about six inches away from the sides of the shed. On these, even in a small shed, an enormous amount of herbs can be dried. Drying herbs by spreading them out on a table is slow and involves far more trouble than putting up strings, for the herbs have to be turned at least twice a day. In a summer like that of 1940 with long spells of drought, drying conditions are ideal, but sometimes in July and August we have a good deal of rain, and in a really wet summer drying can be done only with such difficulty that it is simpler to dry them in the oven. In cold parts it is rarely possible to dry effectively except in the oven. The best way is to remove the oven shelves, balance rods across, resting the ends of them on the shelf supports, and tying the bunches of herbs to these. Oven drying has to be done in a very cool oven.

MODERN METHOD OF DRYING HERBS

I am always ready to learn new-fangled ways, but in my experience this method is no better than the old-fashioned way and takes longer. Small-leaved herbs, such as Winter Savory and Thyme, cannot be dried by this method, for it is suitable only for large-leaved herbs, such as Mint. Pick the leaves from the stalks, wash them, tie them up in muslin, and dip in boiling water. Shake off all superfluous moisture, spread the leaves out on trays, and place in a cool oven (110–130° F.). Dry till the leaves are perfectly crisp. The time taken is about an hour. If the herbs are placed in a very warm place above the stove, it takes about a day. When dry rub to powder, put into bottles, and cork securely.

CHAPTER IV

USES OF HERBS

HERBS may not be "food" in the popular sense of the word, but they are in reality, for they contain salts invaluable to health, so in this respect they compare favourably with the bought sauces which all good French cooks regard with scorn. There is certainly no comparison between dishes flavoured with herbs and the same dishes flavoured with bought sauces. And it is noteworthy that it is the cheaper dishes that are so much improved by herbs. For instance, an old fowl boiled gently with leeks, a few prunes, rice, seasoning, and herbs is a dish that recalls the days when farmhouse cooking was noted. Old partridges stewed with a small savoy cabbage, onion and carrot, a little bacon, salt and pepper, a tablespoonful of chopped thyme, parsley, and balm is excellent, but omit the herbs and the dish would lack character. A cheap cut of beef stewed with onions, potatoes, and herbs makes a savoury meal. Breast of mutton can be made to go much farther by turning it into mock goose —boning the mutton and stuffing it with a mixture of breadcrumbs moistened in milk, a tablespoonful of chopped sage, a tablespoonful of sliced onion, seasoning, and a walnut of margarine. A cheap minced shape made with a pound of minced uncooked meat, a teacupful of breadcrumbs, one egg, and a tablespoonful of chopped herbs is appetising hot or cold. All lentils and dried pea or bean dishes are improved by the addition of herbs.

If bought sauces were used instead of herbs, these dishes would indeed be poor. These are but a few examples, but they could be multiplied indefinitely.

Herbs skilfully used make omelets "with a difference." For instance, finely chopped chives are an ideal flavouring for either omelets or scrambled eggs. A dish sometimes called Scottish Omelet is made thus: Break up four ounces of crustless bread, pour on half a pint of hot milk, and leave soaking for an hour. Beat up well with a fork, add three medium-sized chopped onions, a teaspoonful of finely chopped sage and half as much of thyme and rather less of sweet marjoram, half an ounce of butter, an ounce of coarse oatmeal, seasoning, and, last of all, three well-beaten eggs. Put the mixture in a greased shallow dish and bake for about an hour.

The addition of chopped herbs transforms mere tomato juice. To a pint of tomato juice allow one tablespoonful of orange juice and two of lemon juice, a teaspoonful of very finely chopped basil, chives, tarragon, and winter savory leaves, a teaspoonful of white sugar, a pinch of cayenne, and a saltspoonful of salt. Make several hours before it is needed and strain before serving.

Herb Puddings (to serve with roast meat)

(1) To a teacupful of fine oatmeal allow two teacupfuls of breadcrumbs. Pour a pint of hot milk over these ingredients and leave for about ten minutes. Beat in an egg. Add four ounces of chopped suet or an equal quantity of margarine. Add half a pound of finely chopped onions, seasoning, a teaspoonful of dried herbs.

Mix all ingredients and put in a Yorkshire pudding tin and bake for about an hour.

(2) This is a well-known Westmorland recipe, and is there called Easter Pudding because one of the chief ingredients is *Polygonum bistorta,* popularly known as Easter May Giant or Easter Ledges. It is a native plant, but is also cultivated on account of the pleasant flavour of the young shoots. This native herb is not a necessary ingredient, and the pudding can be made at any time of year and is most useful for making meat go farther. To a pint of cooked barley allow two heaping table-spoonfuls of finely chopped herbs and leaves that are at their best in spring—young black-currant leaves, Easter May giant, parsley, mint, dandelion, etc., together with an eggspoonful of finely chopped onion. Add the mixture with seasoning and an egg to the barley and bake in a greased pudding dish. The addition of a little butter or margarine is advisable if rations will run to it.

In midwinter, when few fresh herbs except sage, winter savory, rosemary, lavender, and chervil are available, dried herbs can be used, also spiced salt or pepper (see page 81).

Cheese of the Seven Herbs

This is an old Cumberland recipe, and the name dates back at least two hundred years.

To four ounces of grated cheese allow two tablespoonfuls of thick cream, three tablespoonfuls of sherry, and two level tablespoonfuls of the following herbs in mixture: finely chopped parsley, sage, thyme, tarragon, chives, chervil, and winter savory, also seasoning to taste. Put all the ingredients into a double saucepan and stir over very gentle heat till the mixture is creamy and pale green in colour. Whilst still warm, fill up small pots with the cheese and use when cold.

Herb Butters

Margarine can be made more palatable by using recipes given below. Those numbered one, two, and four can be fairly quickly made.

(1) *Maître d'Hôtel Butter*.—To half an ounce of butter allow a few drops of lemon juice, half a teaspoonful of very finely chopped parsley, a quarter of a teaspoonful of very finely chopped chervil and seasoning. Beat the butter to a cream, add the other ingredients. Serve in tiny squares in a dish or in one large square on the top of steak, etc.

(2) *Mint Butter*.—Exactly the same way as Maître d'Hôtel Butter, substituting mint for parsley (see also under Mint, page 44). Any herbs, balm, fennel, basil, winter savory, thyme, sage, tarragon, watercress, etc., can be used. Excellent for sandwiches.

(3) *Green Butter*.—This was a favourite delicacy in Victorian days. To an ounce of butter allow a quarter of a clove of garlic, one shallot, one sprig of watercress, one spray of chervil, three sprays of parsley, a saltspoonful of salt, and a pinch of cayenne pepper. Pound all the ingredients (except the butter) in a mortar till reduced to a pulp. Add the butter and pound again. Rub through a very fine sieve and keep in a cold place till required.

(4) *Shallot Butter*.—To a quarter of a pound of butter allow a heaping teaspoonful of very finely chopped shallot, an eggspoonful of mustard, the juice of a

medium-sized lemon, seasoning, and a pinch of cayenne pepper. Beat well together. For variety add yolks of boiled eggs rubbed smooth and a little tomato juice. Excellent with wholemeal bread.

(5) *Beurre de Montpellier.*—To half a pound of butter allow a handful of tarragon, chervil, chives, and two spring onions when obtainable. Boil them for two minutes in salted water to keep the colour green. Drain thoroughly and pound to a pulp in a mortar. Add the yolks to two boiled eggs, a few capers, a quarter of a clove of garlic, a pinch of mustard, a pinch of cayenne, and seasoning. Pound all together till perfectly smooth. Add the butter and a teaspoonful of tarragon vinegar. Rub through a fine sieve. This butter should be green, and if not green enough, make a " greening " with spinach or parsley. Pound a sufficient quantity in a mortar and press the juice through a cloth. Warm it, but do not let it boil. Strain and use enough to colour the butter.

Herb Vinegars

(1) *Vinegar flavoured with Mixed Herbs.*—To a gallon of the best wine vinegar allow four ounces each of chives, shallots, tarragon, winter savory, and balm and a good handful of mint. Pound to a pulp. Put all into the vinegar, cork well, and place in the sun every day for a fortnight. At the end of that time strain, squeezing the herbs in doing so. Leave to settle for a few hours, and then strain through a fine cloth and bottle.

(2) *Shallot Vinegar.*—Cut up eight shallots, put them into a bottle, and fill up with the best wine vinegar. Cork well. Fit for use in a month's time.

(3) *Tarragon Vinegar.*—Tarragon to be used for vinegar should be gathered in July and, in any case, before it flowers. Gather when there has been no rain for at least two days. Pick the leaves off the stalks and put them in a bottle, pour in the vinegar. Allow eight ounces of the leaves to two quarts of vinegar. Cork well and leave for a fortnight. Strain, bottle again, and cork well.

(4) *Basil Vinegar.*—Made as above.

(5) *Chervil Vinegar.*—Made as above.

(6) *Elder-flower Vinegar.*—Made as above. The sprays of flowers should be gathered when almost fully open.

Spiced Pepper

To half an ounce of black pepper allow half an ounce of powdered mace and two ounces of dried rosemary, thyme, sweet marjoram, and winter savory (half an ounce of each dried herb). Pass through a fine sieve and bottle.

Spiced Salt

To four ounces of salt allow one ounce of spiced pepper made as above. Store in a well-corked bottle.

Herb Teas

The herb teas so commonly made even as late as our great-grandmothers' days are most wholesome, and might well be revived. They can be made from the following garden herbs: Alecost, Angelica, Balm, Bergamot, Dandelion, Dill, Hyssop, Lavender, Lovage, Marjoram, Marigold petals, Mints, Parsley, Rosemary, Sage, Savories, Sweet Cicely, and Thymes.

The quantities are half a pint of boiling water poured on to a good handful of the leaves of any of the herbs mentioned above. An overdose is perfectly harmless, but nothing is gained by taking an excess of herb teas. Half a pint of any one of them or half a pint made from a mixture of them is sufficient each day. Dried herbs are very concentrated, and not more than a level teaspoonful should be used in making the tea. Certain herbs have such a strong flavour that less quantities should be used. For instance, three sprays of Rue leaves are sufficient instead of a handful. In olden times certain herb teas were taken regularly in their season. Sage tea in May, Parsley tea in summer, and so forth.

In the making of herb teas, it is important to keep the infusions covered to prevent the escape of steam.

See also under the various herbs.

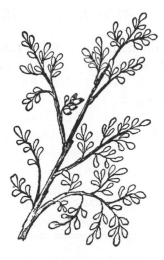

RUE

SAGE

BORAGE

BALM

CHAPTER V

SALADS

A SALAD lacking the flavouring of herbs is a dull affair. We use about twenty in our salads, chopping up a piled tablespoonful very finely and mixing it in. The variety of flavours is great—the pungent Basil, the strong aromatic sweetness of Sweet Marjoram, the anise-like flavour of Sweet Cicely, the pleasant taste of Lovage (rather like Parsley and Celery combined), the unusual flavour of Alecost, the fragrant Mints, the cordial Sage, Winter Savory, Hyssop, and Thyme, the suspicion of Onion afforded by Chives, the lemon flavour of Balm, the nutty taste of Purslane, the indescribable scent and taste of Fennel, the pleasant flavour of Tarragon, Dill, and Angelica leaves. Even such pungent leaves as Rue can be used, but these powerful flavours have to be used with discretion. As much finely chopped Rue as will cover a threepenny piece is quite enough, and Sweet Marjoram and the Basils if overdone will dominate the salad. In a heaping tablespoonful of roughly cut up herbs we allow only one leaflet of Rue and a leaf or so of Sweet Marjoram and the Basils. It is just the suspicion of flavouring all through the salad that is required, not a salad entirely dominated by herbs.

Certain ingredients, such as Lettuce, Celery, Radish, Beet, Endive, Chives, Watercress, Tomato, Corn Salad, and Cucumber, are commonly used, but why not use also finely shredded Brussels Sprouts, Dandelion, Beet tops, Turnip tops, Good King Henry, finely shredded or grated Carrots, Turnips, Beet, Horse-radish, Hamburg Parsley root, grated Celeriac, Swede, and Onion, young Celery tops, grated Cauliflower or Broccoli, Orach, Chinese Mustard, Asparagus Peas? To these may be added grated orange and lemon peel (frequently wasted in spite of their health-giving qualities and flavour), pineapple, grated nuts, raisins, sultanas, sliced dates, grated or sliced apple, sliced prunes.

Flowers in Salads

And why do we make so little use of flowers in salads? Rose petals, Nasturtiums, Sage flowers, Bergamot, Anchusa, Borage, Marigolds, Rosemary, and Lavender are some of the best edible flowers. It is a pity to waste Rose petals when they are going to drop, for they are particularly wholesome. Marigold petals too have very health-giving properties. The idea of eating flowers is disliked by some people, yet they do not hesitate to wear flowers and use flower essences for scents, etc., and I can see no real difference. Personally, I would rather eat a few flower petals than wear flowers and see them die slowly. Flower petals strewn in mixture over a salad make it look very gay, and for a change try chopping finely a few tablespoonfuls of mixed petals. It gives a salad a carnival look.

Salads of Cold Cooked Vegetables

Nor are we as a nation sufficiently appreciative of salads made of cold cooked vegetables. Cold Potatoes, Carrots, Turnips, Beet, Peas, Asparagus Peas, Celery,

Beans of any sort, separately, still better in mixture, masked with a little mayonnaise sauce and decorated with chopped Parsley, Winter Savory, or paprika, are as delicious as they are attractive in appearance.   Further, salads are an excellent way of using up all sorts of scraps.   Meat and fish should, of course, never figure together in salad, but otherwise all sorts of " bits " can go in.   Left-overs of omelet, savoury dishes, such as macaroni cheese, cut into neat squares, all make variety.   Nor is there any reason why green saladings and cold root vegetables should not be mixed.   Given the inclusion of an adequate amount of protein in the shape of meat, fish, cheese, or nuts, a salad can form the staple dish every day for luncheon, and owing to the large variety of saladings obtainable, there need be no monotony.   I think our ancestors would have had a poor opinion of the few ingredients that compose the average modern salad. James II's head cook considered that there should be at least thirty-two ingredients, and a " brave sallet " contained more than that, for it was the decorative centre-piece of the table.   John Evelyn gave it as his considered opinion that he " could by no means approve the extravagant Fancy of some who tell us that a Fool is as fit to be the gatherer of Sallets as a wise man," and his ideal housewife numbered amongst her virtues that she " could in a trice set forth an handsome sallet."   She must have been a remarkable woman, for those of us with practical experience know that making an elaborate salad takes time.   On the other hand, there is no doubt that the salad luncheon daily, followed by fruits or a very simple sweet, does solve the problem of this meal in two

ways. Firstly, though it may take a little time to make a
good salad (though a little experience soon accelerates
matters), on the other hand, it is far simpler to use up
any scraps of protein, as suggested above, in a salad than
to rack one's brain as to how to use remains to make
cooked dishes; and secondly, consider the little amount of
washing up a salad meal involves.

The Food Value of Salads

In the matter of food values we are returning to the
wisdom of the ancients. Hippocrates, "the Father of
Medicine," laid down the axiom, "Make food your
medicine and medicine your food." In other words, eat
foods that make and keep you well. The health of a
nation is its greatest source of true wealth, and it is small
wonder that the ancient Greeks regarded a knowledge of
food values as a matter of primary importance.

How should we eat to ensure health? The answer is
laid down in the leading scientific diets, namely to eat a
balanced diet—that is to say, a diet consisting of 75 per
cent. alkali-forming foods (fruit and vegetables) and 25
per cent. acid-forming foods (most of the proteins and
starchy foods). Further, the 75 per cent. alkali-forming
food should consist of both raw and cooked vegetables,
and fruit always raw, because the chemical balance of
fruit is very delicate and so easily upset that cooking
makes it acid- instead of alkali-forming. The majority
of people in this country eat food that is preponderatingly
acid-forming, with the result that they fall a prey to

countless ills. Further, it is of the utmost importance that the vegetables and fruits eaten should be grown on natural and not artificial manures, for grown on artificials, they lack the health-giving qualities of those grown on natural manures.

Why is it that in all scientific diets so much emphasis is laid on the importance of eating daily, summer and winter alike, a large salad in which greenstuff predominates? Because all green or leafy vegetables are the richest in vitamins and contain valuable salts which are lost in the usual methods of cooking.

All vegetables are health-giving, and it is therefore obvious that the ideal salad should contain ingredients of all the various classes of vegetables. For practical purposes saladings may be divided into three classes:

(1) Green vegetables, i.e. vegetables of which the leafy tops are eaten—Dandelion, Endive, Lettuce, Curly Kale, Spinach, Watercress, Cabbage, Beet tops, Turnip tops, etc. Unfortunately, some of the most valuable leaves are those least commonly eaten, notably Dandelion, Endive, Parsley, Curly Kale, and Turnip tops, the outer leaves of Lettuce, Cabbage, and Cauliflower. Outer leaves are anything from twice to five times as rich in vitamins as the hearts. They are in every way the most valuable because they have had the maximum exposure to sunlight. Tender bleached hearts contain very little Vitamin A. French peasants, and in past times our own country-folk, knew very well from practical experience the health-giving properties of Dandelions. In France the leaves are regularly harvested and sold, whereas in this country it is almost impossible to buy the leaves. Dandelion is rich in Vitamin A and has four times as

much Vitamin C as Lettuce. In common with other bitter-leaved plants, such as Endive, it is rich in potassium. And Dandelion is slightly richer than Spinach in iron. Curly Kale is very rich in salts, and though the leaves are too tough to eat whole, the curly edges can be chopped up as easily as Parsley. Parsley, in spite of its health-giving qualities, is almost invariably used merely as a decoration. Our ancestors, however, were keenly aware of its health-giving properties, especially for all forms of rheumatism. Parsley is as rich in Vitamin A as some grades of Cod-liver Oil, and amongst edible leaves comes second only to Spinach and Turnip tops in this respect. In Vitamin C Parsley is richer than any other food—three times as rich as oranges. Spinach and Turnip tops are almost always cooked and it takes very little overcooking to destroy Vitamin C. When in season, Spinach and Turnip tops should be finely snipped up and added to salads. Turnip tops are specially rich in calcium and are slightly richer in iron than Good King Henry, Spinach, or Beet tops. The outer leaves of Cabbage are most unpalatable when cooked, and in any case much reduced in value by cooking, but a small quantity, finely snipped up, of the raw leaves—a handful, for instance—should, like Spinach and Turnip tops, be added to salads. Incidentally, if cabbages are cooked, as is still done in many houses, with a pinch of soda " to improve the colour," their value is wholly destroyed and they are reduced to mere roughage. Green Celery leaves are more valuable than the blanched stalks, and should be finely chopped up with other green leaves for the salad bowl.

(2) Root vegetables, such as Carrots, Turnips, Ham-

burg Parsley, Beet, etc. Raw Carrot is very easily
digested, and this vegetable is rich in potash, magnesium,
lime, and iron. In Parsnips lime, magnesium, and
potassium are the most important salts. Radishes abound
in lime, iron, sulphur, and potassium. Turnips are rich
in sulphur. Raw sulphur has wonderful curative
powers, but cooking sulphur makes it very indigestible,
and it is for this reason that many people find Cabbages,
Turnips, and Onions impossible to digest. All the root
vegetables are very palatable when grated raw, but
grated Turnip, Beet, Onion, and Horse-radish are very
" hot " and can be added only in small quantities.

(3) Flower-heads, such as Cauliflower, Calabrese,
Broccoli, etc., are as rich in Vitamin C as orange juice.
Like green vegetables, flower-heads depreciate rapidly
after gathering, and should be used as fresh as possible.

It is, indeed, a matter of the utmost importance that
the ingredients of the salad bowl should be really fresh.
If Lettuces, etc., are gathered in the early morning and
not served till luncheon, they are not fresh. They have
been losing vitality all those hours, and that loss is not
improved by the prolonged soaking in salted water to
which they are usually subjected. Twenty minutes is the
longest any green vegetable should be left in salted water.
There is no comparison between the flavour and health-
giving qualities of, for instance, a Lettuce cut, washed,
and served within twenty minutes and one that is several
hours old. In the life of a Lettuce a few hours is a very
long time. Townsfolk have no chance of tasting really
fresh Lettuces, etc., and it is small wonder that they
eat so little of the inferior salads to which they are
accustomed. An American friend told me that she

attended a series of lectures on diet by one of their leading authorities, and he was emphatic on the point that,
for the sake of their health, children should be given
salads straight from the garden to the table, with only
just sufficient time for washing. Lettuces, etc., that are
a refrigerator release are not the same as genuinely fresh
Lettuces. If it is essential to keep Lettuces, Cauliflowers,
etc., for some hours, or, as is necessary in some house-
holds, for perhaps a day or two, the best way is to hang
them up in a piece of dripping-wet butter muslin with
the four corners tied together in some cool and preferably
dark place. At intervals of about eight hours, the whole
should be dipped in a bowl of cold water and then hung
up again. Never hang in a draught, for this dries the
muslin quickly. This method is better than putting the
Lettuces, etc., in water, for in water they deteriorate far
more rapidly and soon become flabby. I have known
Lettuces keep firm for four days hung up in wet butter
muslin dipped in cold water morning and evening.
Should you have the misfortune to be a town-dweller,
the best way of securing Lettuces as fresh as possible is
to buy them early, wash them at once, and hang them up
in butter muslin as described above. You will thereby
secure a Lettuce that is anyhow much fresher than stuff
that has lain about, first at the greengrocer's, and secondly
in the scullery. Another important point is that green
salading should not be crushed or even bruised. The
right way to dry leaves of Lettuce, Endive, etc., is to
swing them vigorously in a butter-muslin cloth. Air
penetrates butter muslin easily, and the leaves, if swung
really vigorously, dry quickly and perfectly. Even
slightly bruised raw leaves are poor stuff.

Making a Salad

It is best to mix a salad in a bowl.   At the bottom put the dressing, arrange the salad on top, and serve.   The dressing should not be incorporated until just before serving, and in some houses this is done at the table by whoever is most skilled at "tossing" a salad.   For a very simple dressing allow three parts oil to one part vinegar or lemon juice, and a pinch of sugar and seasoning.   Some assert that a salad should be tossed in oil first, but oil coats the leaves, etc., and it is impossible for the lemon juice or vinegar to penetrate them.

Do not add flowers to a salad before incorporating the dressing unless the petals are finely chopped and mixed with the other ingredients.   If whole flowers are to figure on a salad, it is best to incorporate the dressing and to arrange the flowers, such as Nasturtium, Rosemary, Anchusa, etc., just before the meal.

Salad Dressings

Vinegar is forbidden in most scientific diets, and lemon juice has to be substituted.   If vinegar is used, it should be the best wine vinegar, and on no account malt vinegar, which is harsh and extremely acid. There is considerable difficulty now in securing olive-oil.

French Dressing

To a tablespoonful of the best wine vinegar (tarragon vinegar may be substituted) allow three of olive-oil. Add seasoning, a pinch of sugar, and a little French mustard (mustard made with good vinegar).   Three drops (not more) of Worcester sauce adds piquancy. For variety add finely chopped tarragon, or chervil or shallot or winter savory or fennel. Or a tablespoonful of tomato purée made with fresh tomatoes.

Simple Salad Dressing

To a saltspoonful of salt add a shake of pepper and a minute pinch of sugar. Mix these ingredients with one tablespoonful of lemon juice (or vinegar). Pour this over the salad and incorporate thoroughly. Then pour a tablespoonful of oil into the bowl and toss the salad ingredients till every leaf and piece of root vegetable, etc., is coated with the dressing.

Salad Dressings without Oil

(1) One dessertspoonful of minced onion, one dessertspoonful of chopped green tarragon, or a few drops of tarragon vinegar, one teaspoonful of salt, half a saltspoonful of cayenne, half a pint of *unsweetened* condensed milk, a few drops of vinegar. Pound the salt, pepper, onion, and tarragon to a paste, add the condensed milk, and mix well, then beat in very gradually about ten drops of vinegar. This will keep some time.

(2) Half a teaspoonful of yeast extract, two tablespoonfuls cream, one tablespoonful of tarragon vinegar, a little pepper, salt, and made mustard, two teaspoonfuls of capers. Mix all well together and dress a salad just before serving.

(3) One hard-boiled egg, two teaspoonfuls of dry mustard, two teaspoonfuls of salt; half a pint of vinegar (tarragon or chili for taste), one tin of *sweet* Nestlé's milk. Boil egg hard and pound the yolk only, mixing

it to the mustard and salt, and then adding the Swiss milk. Lastly the vinegar, stirring the whole thing all the time. Pour into bottles and cork down for use.

(4) Make a roux with a dessertspoonful of flour and a good walnut of margarine. Cook together for three or four minutes to a perfectly smooth paste. Add seasoning. Then add slowly barely half a pint of milk and water. Bring slowly to the boil and boil for about four minutes, stirring well. Add a teaspoonful of made mustard and the juice of two large lemons. If five tablespoonfuls of vinegar are used instead of lemon, this dressing can be bottled when cold.

(5) To three parts of sweet condensed milk allow two parts of vinegar or lemon juice and seasoning to taste. To a quarter pint of the mixture allow half a teaspoonful of made mustard. Put the milk in a bowl, add the seasoning and mustard, and mix well. Then add the vinegar or lemon juice very slowly, beating well. If vinegar is used, this dressing can be bottled.

American Salad Dressing

Two heaped tablespoonfuls of flour, one tablespoonful of butter, mixed well together, one large cupful of brown sugar, half a pint of vinegar, mustard, pepper, and salt to taste. Put into a lined saucepan and stir till it thickens. When cool, break in two whole eggs and a breakfastcupful of milk. Beat all together and bottle.

Russian Salad Dressing

Rub the yolks of two hard-boiled eggs through a sieve. Add seasoning and thin to the desired consistency with sour cream.

Salad Cream (to store)

Mix thoroughly a teaspoonful of flour, half a tea-spoonful of salt, four teaspoonfuls of dry mustard, four teaspoonfuls of olive-oil. When mixed, add two ounces of powdered sugar. Beat up an egg in a pint of milk and stir gradually into the above mixture. Then add, drop by drop, a pint of vinegar. Pour into a saucepan, bring to the boil, stirring continually, and cook for a few minutes till the cream has thickened enough. When quite cold, bottle. This cream keeps well.

If it is impossible to use vinegar, make a small quantity at a time, substituting lemon juice for vinegar. Made with lemon juice, it does not keep.

Salad Dressing (to store)

Mix the yolks of two raw eggs with a teaspoonful of salt and beat thoroughly. Add, drop by drop, a pint of olive-oil. If done hurriedly, it will curdle. When thoroughly incorporated, add one tablespoonful of freshly made mustard, one tablespoonful of tarragon mustard (see page 50), three tablespoonfuls of white vinegar, a pinch of cayenne pepper. Mix thoroughly and bottle.

If impossible to use vinegar, make in small quantities, substituting lemon juice for vinegar, but in this case the dressing will not keep.

An Economical Salad Cream

An inexpensive salad cream that will be found to keep well is made as follows: one and a half teaspoonfuls of salt, one teaspoonful of pepper, two teaspoonfuls of sugar, one teaspoonful of dry mustard, one tablespoonful of olive-oil. Mix these ingredients smoothly together and add two tablespoonfuls of vinegar. Put a large tin-ful of unsweetened milk into a bowl and slowly add the mixed ingredients, stirring all the time. Ordinary milk can be added if needful, and the flavour can be varied by tarragon vinegar.

Cream Salad Dressing

One hard-boiled yolk of egg, two tablespoonfuls of cream, one dessertspoonful of vinegar, half a teaspoonful of made mustard, pinch each of sugar, pepper, and salt. Sieve the yolk into bowl, add the seasonings, and mix in cream by degrees; when it is a smooth paste, gradually work in the vinegar.

MAYONNAISE

There are many variations of this excellent salad dress-ing. The only drawback is that mayonnaise takes quite half- to three-quarters of an hour to make, and any attempt at hurrying matters merely results in curdling.

Allow one yolk to every gill of oil. Beat the yolk with an eggspoonful of dry mustard, a minute pinch of pepper, and a pinch of salt. Add a dessertspoonful of lemon juice or good vinegar. Beat again. Now patiently add the oil, literally drop by drop, stirring the whole time. By the time the sauce is really thick, the oil can be added a little more quickly, though good cooks do not approve of this. A well-made mayonnaise is so smooth that it has a glossy look.

Eggless Mayonnaise

To a tablespoonful of thick cream allow two of oil. Mix the cream with a good pinch of mustard and one of sugar and then add the oil slowly, beating well. When quite thick, add to this sauce a dessertspoonful of lemon juice or vinegar. Beat again.

Cream Mayonnaise

Make the mayonnaise as above, using half cream and half oil, or two parts cream and one part oil. First whip the cream to which seasoning and a pinch of mustard has been added. Do not whip the cream too stiff. Add the oil slowly and whip again. Add lemon juice or vinegar in the proportion of a tablespoonful of lemon juice or tarragon vinegar (see page 81) to a gill of the sauce.

Horse-radish Mayonnaise

Add very finely grated horse-radish and a pinch of sugar in the proportion of a teaspoonful to a gill of oil.

Green-pea Mayonnaise

Make a purée of cooked green peas and add to the mayonnaise in the proportion of a tablespoonful to half a gill of the oil used. Mix the purée with a little cream before adding to the mayonnaise.

Tomato Mayonnaise

Make a purée of uncooked tomatoes, mix with a little cream, and add to the mayonnaise.

Tartare Sauce

Make in the same way as mayonnaise, but use the yolks of hard-boiled eggs and tarragon vinegar (see page 81).

Potato Salads

The cheese, nuts, meat, or fish should be omitted from the following recipes if these foods are served separately. With one of these protein foods included as suggested, any of the following potato salads make a substantial meal. An allowance of two ounces for each person of grated cheese or of the other protein foods mentioned is the maximum that is necessary, this allowance being sufficient for people doing heavy manual work.

New or waxy potatoes are generally supposed to be the best for salads, but many people find them indigestible, and there is no reason why floury old potatoes should not be used. They need careful handling to prevent breaking. If a dressing is used, it should be put on at least an hour before serving, to enable the flavour to penetrate the potatoes. A still better salad is made by slicing the potatoes whilst they are still hot and putting the dressing over them at once. The flavour penetrates far better than with cold potatoes. In view of the difficulty of obtaining either good olive-oil or cream, a substitute dressing can be made by using two parts top creamy milk to one part lemon juice or good vinegar with seasoning, a pinch of mustard, and finely chopped chives, winter savory, parsley, Welsh onion or thyme. Very finely chopped garlic is appreciated by some people, but even so, only very little should be used, just enough to give the required garlic flavour. To three tablespoonfuls of dressing a quarter of a clove (not whole bulb) of garlic is sufficient. The addition of grated cheese or ground nuts makes a substantial meal.

For Dressings see page 92. Allow a quarter of a pint of dressing to two pints of salad.

(1) To four breakfastcupfuls of sliced cooked potatoes allow a small finely grated raw onion, two tomatoes, six prunes (soaked previously in water for twenty-four hours, not cooked prunes), one tablespoonful of raw grated turnip or swede, a tablespoonful of chopped parsley and seasonings. For dressing, add sufficient cold cooked herring, boned and flaked (two ounces for each person), or any cold fish.

(2) To four breakfastcupfuls of sliced cooked potatoes allow one of grated raw beetroot, one teacupful of cold cooked runner beans or cubed cold cooked carrots, a small finely grated raw onion, one tablespoonful of chopped parsley, and seasoning. Add grated cheese (two ounces for each person).

(3) To four breakfastcupfuls of sliced cooked potatoes allow a cupful of chopped celery, four apples (peeled, cored, and thinly sliced), a cupful of grated raw carrot, a cupful of cold cooked and sliced beetroot, a dessertspoonful of mixed herbs finely chopped (see page 84), and seasoning. Add ground nuts (two ounces for each person).

(4) To four breakfastcupfuls of sliced cooked potatoes allow a cup of cold cooked peas or broad beans, a very small finely grated onion, a tablespoonful of finely sliced raw cabbage and seasoning, and the remains of any meat diced.

Potato and Fruit Salad

Potatoes can also figure in rather more " exotic " salads. Cut oranges in half and remove enough rind from the under part to make them stand firmly. Scoop out all the pulp, remove pips, and mix pulp with cooked, rather floury, potato. Fill centres with this mixture. Mask with mayonnaise and decorate with tiny sprays of parsley or watercress. Arrange on a dish with a surround of cup-like lettuce leaves, or failing these small inner Savoy leaves.

Asparagus Salad

Arrange cold cooked asparagus heads in cup-like lettuce leaves. Dress with mayonnaise sauce and decorate with small sprays of chervil.

Autumn or Winter Salad

Take equal quantities of raw celery, cold cooked turnips, and cold cooked carrots. Cut the celery into inch lengths and the turnips and carrots into cubes. Add chopped chives and chopped parsley. Toss together with any good salad dressing. Pile on a dish and sprinkle with finely chopped parsley or chervil.

Beetroot Salad

Skin a cooked beetroot and slice it thinly or thickly as desired. Cover with French dressing to which grated horse-radish has been added.

Chicory Salad

This is excellent for midwinter. Take the outer leaves off the blanched heads. Slice the remainder very finely. Serve with a good dressing (see page 92) or horse-radish mayonnaise. Decorate with chopped parsley or winter savory.

Cabbage Salad

Remove all the leafy parts from the cabbage stems. Shred these leafy parts very finely. Toss in any good dressing (see page 92), decorate with nasturtium flowers, and arrange in individual portions in small savoy cabbage leaves.

Cucumber Salad

Slice the cucumber very thinly, preferably without paring it. Cover with a dressing of olive-oil and lemon juice with finely chopped dill and chives and leave for three hours before serving. Just before serving add a few uncut leaves of tarragon.

Cucumber, Melon, and Mint Salad

Peel the cucumber and cut in neat squares. Add an equal quantity of melon cut in the same way. Cover with a dressing made with olive-oil and a tablespoonful of equal quantities of finely chopped dill, mint, and tarragon and a very little powdered sugar.

Cucumber and Nasturtium Salad

Slice the cucumber thinly, cover with French dressing (see page 92), and leave for three hours. Just before serving decorate with a circle of nasturtium flowers and very young nasturtium leaves.

Endive, Celery, and Apple Salad

Cut a head of celery into match-like pieces, also an equal quantity of apples. Arrange with a surround of endive leaves and mask the celery and apple with mayonnaise.

Fish Salad

To three cooked herrings, or a similar quantity of other fish, allow half a pound of eating apples, an equal quantity of cold cooked potatoes, a bunch of radishes, a tablespoonful of chopped parsley, chervil, and very finely chopped onion. Cut the potatoes and apples in cubes, flake the fish. Toss all these ingredients in any good salad dressing (see page 92). Arrange in a bowl.

Jellied Vegetable Salad

To a quantity of jelly allow half a pound of cooked potatoes diced or sliced, a few grated raw shallots, a breakfastcupful of cooked green peas and diced cooked carrot and beet, a dessertspoonful of chopped parsley or fennel or winter savory, a teaspoonful of grated raw onion, and seasoning. Toss all the ingredients, except the jelly, with a quarter of a cupful of mayonnaise. Pour the jelly into the mould to a depth of barely half an inch. When perfectly set, add the other ingredients gently. Pour over the remainder of the jelly and leave till quite cold, and set. When ready to serve, dip the mould for a few moments in warm water to make the jelly come out easily. Turn on a dish and garnish with watercress or parsley, and put a surround of sliced tomatoes similarly garnished.

Leek Salad

When leeks are large enough to transplant, there is always a surplus of small ones. Cook these, either by steaming them or boiling in as little water as possible. When quite cold, cover with a dressing made of salad oil, lemon juice, black pepper, and a very little mustard.

Mushroom Jelly Salad

To two pounds of mushrooms allow half a grated onion, a few drops of lemon juice, and seasoning. Simmer together till these ingredients can be rubbed through a sieve. Dissolve half an ounce of leaf gelatine in a little water and add to the sieved ingredients. Pour into a mould. When cold and perfectly set, dip the mould in hot water for a few moments to enable the jelly to be turned out easily. Place in the centre of a dish and surround with cold cooked French beans and sliced tomatoes arranged alternately and dressed with French dressing (see page 92).

Mustard and Cress and Apple Salad

Peel the required number of apples and cut them up into match-like pieces. Arrange neatly in a dish. Squeeze lemon juice over them and then sprinkle with a little seasoning. Cover with the mustard and cress similarly dressed. Put another layer of apples cut and dressed as above and finish with mustard and cress decorated with nasturtium flowers.

Parsnip and Cheese Salad

Skin some cooked parsnips and remove the cores. Cut in neat, very small cubes and cut some cheese in equally small cubes. Toss in any good salad dressing (see page 92) and serve on cup-like lettuce leaves or young savoy leaves.

Tomato Salad

Put the tomatoes in boiling water for a few moments in order to be able to peel them easily. Cut them fairly thick in slices and cover with a dressing of olive-oil, lemon juice, salt, a pinch of powdered sugar, and a tablespoonful of equal quantities of finely chopped sweet basil and chives.

Or alternate the slices of tomato with very finely sliced rings of onion and slices of cold cooked potato, dressed as above.

Salad Sandwiches

Lettuce and Carrot Sandwich

Mix equal quantities of finely shredded lettuce and grated raw carrot. Add a little lemon juice. Spread thin pieces of brown bread with butter or margarine and put between them a layer of cream cheese and then the lettuce and carrot mixture. Add a sprinkling of finely chopped parsley or winter savory or fennel or chervil or chives, or a mixture of these herbs.

Lettuce, Watercress, and Fish Sandwich

Flake any remains of cooked fish. Moisten with mayonnaise or any good salad dressing (see page 92). Add an equal quantity of finely shredded lettuce and watercress. Spread between the slices of bread and butter.

Lettuce, Watercress, and Meat Sandwich

Any cold cooked meat can be used, but cold cooked liver is best. Mince it finely, work into a paste with margarine and seasoning. Chop the watercress finely and mix with the meat paste. Use as a filling for sandwiches.

INDEX

A

Alecost, 10, 11, 81, 84
Anchusa, 10, 12, 85, 92
Angelica, 10, 12, 81, 84
Anise, 10, 15, 16
Asparagus pea, 16

B

Balm, 10, 16, 17, 76, 79, 80, 81, 84
Basils, 10, 17, 18, 77, 79, 81, 84, 104
Bergamot, 10, 19, 81, 84, 85
Borage, 10, 20, 85

C

Caraway, 20
Chervil, 10, 20, 78, 79, 80, 81, 93, 100
Chives, 10, 21, 22, 77, 78, 80, 84, 98, 100, 101, 104
Coriander, 10, 22
Corn salad, 23, 24, 25
Cress, 49, 103
Cumin, 25, 26

D

Dandelion, 26, 27, 78, 81, 84, 88, 89
Dill, 10, 28, 29

F

Fennel, 10, 29, 30, 79, 84, 93, 104
    ,,   Florence, 29, 30

G

Garlic, 30, 31, 32, 98

H

Herbs, drying of, 74
    ,,   uses of, 76 *et seq.*
    ,,   General uses : Herb Butters, Herb Puddings (to serve with roast meat), Herb Vinegars, Spiced Pepper, Spiced Salt, Herb Teas
Horse-radish, 32, 33, 34, 85, 90, 97, 100
Hyssop, 34, 35, 81, 84

L

Lavender, 35, 36, 37, 81, 85
Lovage, 37, 81, 84

M

Marigold, 10, 38, 39, 40, 81, 85
Marjoram, pot, 40
    ,,   sweet, 40, 77, 81, 84

A CATALOGUE OF SELECTED DOVER BOOKS
IN ALL FIELDS OF INTEREST

A CATALOGUE OF SELECTED DOVER BOOKS
IN ALL FIELDS OF INTEREST

AMERICA'S OLD MASTERS, James T. Flexner. Four men emerged unexpectedly from provincial 18th century America to leadership in European art: Benjamin West, J. S. Copley, C. R. Peale, Gilbert Stuart. Brilliant coverage of lives and contributions. Revised, 1967 edition. 69 plates. 365pp. of text.

21806-6 Paperbound $3.00

FIRST FLOWERS OF OUR WILDERNESS: AMERICAN PAINTING, THE COLONIAL PERIOD, James T. Flexner. Painters, and regional painting traditions from earliest Colonial times up to the emergence of Copley, West and Peale Sr., Foster, Gustavus Hesselius, Feke, John Smibert and many anonymous painters in the primitive manner. Engaging presentation, with 162 illustrations. xxii + 368pp.

22180-6 Paperbound $3.50

THE LIGHT OF DISTANT SKIES: AMERICAN PAINTING, 1760-1835, James T. Flexner. The great generation of early American painters goes to Europe to learn and to teach: West, Copley, Gilbert Stuart and others. Allston, Trumbull, Morse; also contemporary American painters—primitives, derivatives, academics—who remained in America. 102 illustrations. xiii + 306pp. 22179-2 Paperbound $3.00

A HISTORY OF THE RISE AND PROGRESS OF THE ARTS OF DESIGN IN THE UNITED STATES, William Dunlap. Much the richest mine of information on early American painters, sculptors, architects, engravers, miniaturists, etc. The only source of information for scores of artists, the major primary source for many others. Unabridged reprint of rare original 1834 edition, with new introduction by James T. Flexner, and 394 new illustrations. Edited by Rita Weiss. 6⅝ x 9⅝.

21695-0, 21696-9, 21697-7 Three volumes, Paperbound $13.50

EPOCHS OF CHINESE AND JAPANESE ART, Ernest F. Fenollosa. From primitive Chinese art to the 20th century, thorough history, explanation of every important art period and form, including Japanese woodcuts; main stress on China and Japan, but Tibet, Korea also included. Still unexcelled for its detailed, rich coverage of cultural background, aesthetic elements, diffusion studies, particularly of the historical period. 2nd, 1913 edition. 242 illustrations. lii + 439pp. of text.

20364-6, 20365-4 Two volumes, Paperbound $6.00

THE GENTLE ART OF MAKING ENEMIES, James A. M. Whistler. Greatest wit of his day deflates Oscar Wilde, Ruskin, Swinburne; strikes back at inane critics, exhibitions, art journalism; aesthetics of impressionist revolution in most striking form. Highly readable classic by great painter. Reproduction of edition designed by Whistler. Introduction by Alfred Werner. xxxvi + 334pp.

21875-9 Paperbound $2.50

VISUAL ILLUSIONS: THEIR CAUSES, CHARACTERISTICS, AND APPLICATIONS, Matthew Luckiesh. Thorough description and discussion of optical illusion, geometric and perspective, particularly; size and shape distortions, illusions of color, of motion; natural illusions; use of illusion in art and magic, industry, etc. Most useful today with op art, also for classical art. Scores of effects illustrated. Introduction by William H. Ittleson. 100 illustrations. xxi + 252pp.

21530-X Paperbound $2.00

A HANDBOOK OF ANATOMY FOR ART STUDENTS, Arthur Thomson. Thorough, virtually exhaustive coverage of skeletal structure, musculature, etc. Full text, supplemented by anatomical diagrams and drawings and by photographs of undraped figures. Unique in its comparison of male and female forms, pointing out differences of contour, texture, form. 211 figures, 40 drawings, 86 photographs. xx + 459pp. 5⅜ x 8⅜.

21163-0 Paperbound $3.50

150 MASTERPIECES OF DRAWING, Selected by Anthony Toney. Full page reproductions of drawings from the early 16th to the end of the 18th century, all beautifully reproduced: Rembrandt, Michelangelo, Dürer, Fragonard, Urs, Graf, Wouwerman, many others. First-rate browsing book, model book for artists. xviii + 150pp. 8⅜ x 11¼.

21032-4 Paperbound $2.50

THE LATER WORK OF AUBREY BEARDSLEY, Aubrey Beardsley. Exotic, erotic, ironic masterpieces in full maturity: Comedy Ballet, Venus and Tannhauser, Pierrot, Lysistrata, Rape of the Lock, Savoy material, Ali Baba, Volpone, etc. This material revolutionized the art world, and is still powerful, fresh, brilliant. With *The Early Work,* all Beardsley's finest work. 174 plates, 2 in color. xiv + 176pp. 8⅛ x 11.

21817-1 Paperbound $3.00

DRAWINGS OF REMBRANDT, Rembrandt van Rijn. Complete reproduction of fabulously rare edition by Lippmann and Hofstede de Groot, completely reedited, updated, improved by Prof. Seymour Slive, Fogg Museum. Portraits, Biblical sketches, landscapes, Oriental types, nudes, episodes from classical mythology—All Rembrandt's fertile genius. Also selection of drawings by his pupils and followers. "Stunning volumes," *Saturday Review.* 550 illustrations. lxxviii + 552pp. 9⅛ x 12¼.

21485-0, 21486-9 Two volumes, Paperbound $7.00

THE DISASTERS OF WAR, Francisco Goya. One of the masterpieces of Western civilization—83 etchings that record Goya's shattering, bitter reaction to the Napoleonic war that swept through Spain after the insurrection of 1808 and to war in general. Reprint of the first edition, with three additional plates from Boston's Museum of Fine Arts. All plates facsimile size. Introduction by Philip Hofer, Fogg Museum. v + 97pp. 9⅜ x 8¼.

21872-4 Paperbound $2.00

GRAPHIC WORKS OF ODILON REDON. Largest collection of Redon's graphic works ever assembled: 172 lithographs, 28 etchings and engravings, 9 drawings. These include some of his most famous works. All the plates from *Odilon Redon: oeuvre graphique complet,* plus additional plates. New introduction and caption translations by Alfred Werner. 209 illustrations. xxvii + 209pp. 9⅛ x 12¼.

21966-8 Paperbound $4.00

A History of Costume, Carl Köhler. Definitive history, based on surviving pieces of clothing primarily, and paintings, statues, etc. secondarily. Highly readable text, supplemented by 594 illustrations of costumes of the ancient Mediterranean peoples, Greece and Rome, the Teutonic prehistoric period; costumes of the Middle Ages, Renaissance, Baroque, 18th and 19th centuries. Clear, measured patterns are provided for many clothing articles. Approach is practical throughout. Enlarged by Emma von Sichart. 464pp. 21030-8 Paperbound $3.50

Oriental Rugs, Antique and Modern, Walter A. Hawley. A complete and authoritative treatise on the Oriental rug—where they are made, by whom and how, designs and symbols, characteristics in detail of the six major groups, how to distinguish them and how to buy them. Detailed technical data is provided on periods, weaves, warps, wefts, textures, sides, ends and knots, although no technical background is required for an understanding. 11 color plates, 80 halftones, 4 maps. vi + 320pp. 6⅛ x 9⅛. 22366-3 Paperbound $5.00

Ten Books on Architecture, Vitruvius. By any standards the most important book on architecture ever written. Early Roman discussion of aesthetics of building, construction methods, orders, sites, and every other aspect of architecture has inspired, instructed architecture for about 2,000 years. Stands behind Palladio, Michelangelo, Bramante, Wren, countless others. Definitive Morris H. Morgan translation. 68 illustrations. xii + 331pp. 20645-9 Paperbound $2.50

The Four Books of Architecture, Andrea Palladio. Translated into every major Western European language in the two centuries following its publication in 1570, this has been one of the most influential books in the history of architecture. Complete reprint of the 1738 Isaac Ware edition. New introduction by Adolf Placzek, Columbia Univ. 216 plates. xxii + 110pp. of text. 9½ x 12¾. 21308-0 Clothbound $10.00

Sticks and Stones: A Study of American Architecture and Civilization, Lewis Mumford.One of the great classics of American cultural history. American architecture from the medieval-inspired earliest forms to the early 20th century; evolution of structure and style, and reciprocal influences on environment. 21 photographic illustrations. 238pp. 20202-X Paperbound $2.00

The American Builder's Companion, Asher Benjamin. The most widely used early 19th century architectural style and source book, for colonial up into Greek Revival periods. Extensive development of geometry of carpentering, construction of sashes, frames, doors, stairs; plans and elevations of domestic and other buildings. Hundreds of thousands of houses were built according to this book, now invaluable to historians, architects, restorers, etc. 1827 edition. 59 plates. 114pp. 7⅞ x 10¾. 22236-5 Paperbound $3.00

Dutch Houses in the Hudson Valley Before 1776, Helen Wilkinson Reynolds. The standard survey of the Dutch colonial house and outbuildings, with constructional features, decoration, and local history associated with individual homesteads. Introduction by Franklin D. Roosevelt. Map. 150 illustrations. 469pp. 6⅝ x 9¼. 21469-9 Paperbound $4.00

THE ARCHITECTURE OF COUNTRY HOUSES, Andrew J. Downing. Together with Vaux's *Villas and Cottages* this is the basic book for Hudson River Gothic architecture of the middle Victorian period. Full, sound discussions of general aspects of housing, architecture, style, decoration, furnishing, together with scores of detailed house plans, illustrations of specific buildings, accompanied by full text. Perhaps the most influential single American architectural book. 1850 edition. Introduction by J. Stewart Johnson. 321 figures, 34 architectural designs. xvi + 560pp.
22003-6 Paperbound $4.00

LOST EXAMPLES OF COLONIAL ARCHITECTURE, John Mead Howells. Full-page photographs of buildings that have disappeared or been so altered as to be denatured, including many designed by major early American architects. 245 plates. xvii + 248pp. 7⅞ x 10¾. 21143-6 Paperbound $3.00

DOMESTIC ARCHITECTURE OF THE AMERICAN COLONIES AND OF THE EARLY REPUBLIC, Fiske Kimball. Foremost architect and restorer of Williamsburg and Monticello covers nearly 200 homes between 1620-1825. Architectural details, construction, style features, special fixtures, floor plans, etc. Generally considered finest work in its area. 219 illustrations of houses, doorways, windows, capital mantels. xx + 314pp. 7⅞ x 10¾. 21743-4 Paperbound $3.50

EARLY AMERICAN ROOMS: 1650-1858, edited by Russell Hawes Kettell. Tour of 12 rooms, each representative of a different era in American history and each furnished, decorated, designed and occupied in the style of the era. 72 plans and elevations, 8-page color section, etc., show fabrics, wall papers, arrangements, etc. Full descriptive text. xvii + 200pp. of text. 8⅜ x 11¼.
21633-0 Paperbound $5.00

THE FITZWILLIAM VIRGINAL BOOK, edited by J. Fuller Maitland and W. B. Squire. Full modern printing of famous early 17th-century ms. volume of 300 works by Morley, Byrd, Bull, Gibbons, etc. For piano or other modern keyboard instrument; easy to read format. xxxvi + 938pp. 8⅜ x 11.
21068-5, 21069-3 Two volumes, Paperbound $8.00

HARPSICHORD MUSIC, Johann Sebastian Bach. Bach Gesellschaft edition. A rich selection of Bach's masterpieces for the harpsichord: the six English Suites, six French Suites, the six Partitas (Clavierübung part I), the Goldberg Variations (Clavierübung part IV), the fifteen Two-Part Inventions and the fifteen Three-Part Sinfonias. Clearly reproduced on large sheets with ample margins; eminently playable. vi + 312pp. 8⅛ x 11. 22360-4 Paperbound $5.00

THE MUSIC OF BACH: AN INTRODUCTION, Charles Sanford Terry. A fine, nontechnical introduction to Bach's music, both instrumental and vocal. Covers organ music, chamber music, passion music, other types. Analyzes themes, developments, innovations. x + 114pp. 21075-8 Paperbound $1.25

BEETHOVEN AND HIS NINE SYMPHONIES, Sir George Grove. Noted British musicologist provides best history, analysis, commentary on symphonies. Very thorough, rigorously accurate; necessary to both advanced student and amateur music lover. 436 musical passages. vii + 407 pp. 20334-4 Paperbound $2.25

JOHANN SEBASTIAN BACH, Philipp Spitta. One of the great classics of musicology, this definitive analysis of Bach's music (and life) has never been surpassed. Lucid, nontechnical analyses of hundreds of pieces (30 pages devoted to St. Matthew Passion, 26 to B Minor Mass). Also includes major analysis of 18th-century music. 450 musical examples. 40-page musical supplement. Total of xx + 1799pp.
(EUK) 22278-0, 22279-9 Two volumes, Clothbound $15.00

MOZART AND HIS PIANO CONCERTOS, Cuthbert Girdlestone. The only full-length study of an important area of Mozart's creativity. Provides detailed analyses of all 23 concertos, traces inspirational sources. 417 musical examples. Second edition. 509pp. (USO) 21271-8 Paperbound $3.50

THE PERFECT WAGNERITE: A COMMENTARY ON THE NIBLUNG'S RING, George Bernard Shaw. Brilliant and still relevant criticism in remarkable essays on Wagner's Ring cycle, Shaw's ideas on political and social ideology behind the plots, role of Leitmotifs, vocal requisites, etc. Prefaces. xxi + 136pp.
21707-8 Paperbound $1.50

DON GIOVANNI, W. A. Mozart. Complete libretto, modern English translation; biographies of composer and librettist; accounts of early performances and critical reaction. Lavishly illustrated. All the material you need to understand and appreciate this great work. Dover Opera Guide and Libretto Series; translated and introduced by Ellen Bleiler. 92 illustrations. 209pp.
21134-7 Paperbound $1.50

HIGH FIDELITY SYSTEMS: A LAYMAN'S GUIDE, Roy F. Allison. All the basic information you need for setting up your own audio system: high fidelity and stereo record players, tape records, F.M. Connections, adjusting tone arm, cartridge, checking needle alignment, positioning speakers, phasing speakers, adjusting hums, trouble-shooting, maintenance, and similar topics. Enlarged 1965 edition. More than 50 charts, diagrams, photos. iv + 91pp. 21514-8 Paperbound $1.25

REPRODUCTION OF SOUND, Edgar Villchur. Thorough coverage for laymen of high fidelity systems, reproducing systems in general, needles, amplifiers, preamps, loudspeakers, feedback, explaining physical background. "A rare talent for making technicalities vividly comprehensible," R. Darrell, *High Fidelity*. 69 figures. iv + 92pp. 21515-6 Paperbound $1.25

HEAR ME TALKIN' TO YA: THE STORY OF JAZZ AS TOLD BY THE MEN WHO MADE IT, Nat Shapiro and Nat Hentoff. Louis Armstrong, Fats Waller, Jo Jones, Clarence Williams, Billy Holiday, Duke Ellington, Jelly Roll Morton and dozens of other jazz greats tell how it was in Chicago's South Side, New Orleans, depression Harlem and the modern West Coast as jazz was born and grew. xvi + 429pp.
21726-4 Paperbound $2.50

FABLES OF AESOP, translated by Sir Roger L'Estrange. A reproduction of the very rare 1931 Paris edition; a selection of the most interesting fables, together with 50 imaginative drawings by Alexander Calder. v + 128pp. 6½x9¼.
21780-9 Paperbound $1.50

POEMS OF ANNE BRADSTREET, edited with an introduction by Robert Hutchinson. A new selection of poems by America's first poet and perhaps the first significant woman poet in the English language. 48 poems display her development in works of considerable variety—love poems, domestic poems, religious meditations, formal elegies, "quaternions," etc. Notes, bibliography. viii + 222pp.

22160-1 Paperbound $2.00

THREE GOTHIC NOVELS: THE CASTLE OF OTRANTO BY HORACE WALPOLE; VATHEK BY WILLIAM BECKFORD; THE VAMPYRE BY JOHN POLIDORI, WITH FRAGMENT OF A NOVEL BY LORD BYRON, edited by E. F. Bleiler. The first Gothic novel, by Walpole; the finest Oriental tale in English, by Beckford; powerful Romantic supernatural story in versions by Polidori and Byron. All extremely important in history of literature; all still exciting, packed with supernatural thrills, ghosts, haunted castles, magic, etc. xl + 291pp.

21232-7 Paperbound $2.00

THE BEST TALES OF HOFFMANN, E. T. A. Hoffmann. 10 of Hoffmann's most important stories, in modern re-editings of standard translations: Nutcracker and the King of Mice, Signor Formica, Automata, The Sandman, Rath Krespel, The Golden Flowerpot, Master Martin the Cooper, The Mines of Falun, The King's Betrothed, A New Year's Eve Adventure. 7 illustrations by Hoffmann. Edited by E. F. Bleiler. xxxix + 419pp.

21793-0 Paperbound $2.50

GHOST AND HORROR STORIES OF AMBROSE BIERCE, Ambrose Bierce. 23 strikingly modern stories of the horrors latent in the human mind: The Eyes of the Panther, The Damned Thing, An Occurrence at Owl Creek Bridge, An Inhabitant of Carcosa, etc., plus the dream-essay, Visions of the Night. Edited by E. F. Bleiler. xxii + 199pp.

20767-6 Paperbound $1.50

BEST GHOST STORIES OF J. S. LEFANU, J. Sheridan LeFanu. Finest stories by Victorian master often considered greatest supernatural writer of all. Carmilla, Green Tea, The Haunted Baronet, The Familiar, and 12 others. Most never before available in the U. S. A. Edited by E. F. Bleiler. 8 illustrations from Victorian publications. xvii + 467pp.

20415-4 Paperbound $2.50

THE TIME STREAM, THE GREATEST ADVENTURE, AND THE PURPLE SAPPHIRE—THREE SCIENCE FICTION NOVELS, John Taine (Eric Temple Bell). Great American mathematician was also foremost science fiction novelist of the 1920's. The Time Stream, one of all-time classics, uses concepts of circular time; The Greatest Adventure, incredibly ancient biological experiments from Antarctica threaten to escape; The Purple Sapphire, superscience, lost races in Central Tibet, survivors of the Great Race. 4 illustrations by Frank R. Paul. v + 532pp.

21180-0 Paperbound $3.00

SEVEN SCIENCE FICTION NOVELS, H. G. Wells. The standard collection of the great novels. Complete, unabridged. First Men in the Moon, Island of Dr. Moreau, War of the Worlds, Food of the Gods, Invisible Man, Time Machine, In the Days of the Comet. Not only science fiction fans, but every educated person owes it to himself to read these novels. 1015pp.

20264-X Clothbound $5.00

THE RED FAIRY BOOK, Andrew Lang. Lang's color fairy books have long been children's favorites. This volume includes Rapunzel, Jack and the Bean-stalk and 35 other stories, familiar and unfamiliar. 4 plates, 93 illustrations x + 367pp.
21673-X Paperbound $2.50

THE BLUE FAIRY BOOK, Andrew Lang. Lang's tales come from all countries and all times. Here are 37 tales from Grimm, the Arabian Nights, Greek Mythology, and other fascinating sources. 8 plates, 130 illustrations. xi + 390pp.
21437-0 Paperbound $2.50

HOUSEHOLD STORIES BY THE BROTHERS GRIMM. Classic English-language edition of the well-known tales — Rumpelstiltskin, Snow White, Hansel and Gretel, The Twelve Brothers, Faithful John, Rapunzel, Tom Thumb (52 stories in all). Translated into simple, straightforward English by Lucy Crane. Ornamented with headpieces, vignettes, elaborate decorative initials and a dozen full-page illustrations by Walter Crane. x + 269pp.
21080-4 Paperbound $2.50

THE MERRY ADVENTURES OF ROBIN HOOD, Howard Pyle. The finest modern versions of the traditional ballads and tales about the great English outlaw. Howard Pyle's complete prose version, with every word, every illustration of the first edition. Do not confuse this facsimile of the original (1883) with modern editions that change text or illustrations. 23 plates plus many page decorations. xxii + 296pp.
22043-5 Paperbound $2.50

THE STORY OF KING ARTHUR AND HIS KNIGHTS, Howard Pyle. The finest children's version of the life of King Arthur; brilliantly retold by Pyle, with 48 of his most imaginative illustrations. xviii + 313pp. 6⅛ x 9¼.
21445-1 Paperbound $2.50

THE WONDERFUL WIZARD OF OZ, L. Frank Baum. America's finest children's book in facsimile of first edition with all Denslow illustrations in full color. The edition a child should have. Introduction by Martin Gardner. 23 color plates, scores of drawings. iv + 267pp.
20691-2 Paperbound $2.25

THE MARVELOUS LAND OF OZ, L. Frank Baum. The second Oz book, every bit as imaginative as the Wizard. The hero is a boy named Tip, but the Scarecrow and the Tin Woodman are back, as is the Oz magic. 16 color plates, 120 drawings by John R. Neill. 287pp.
20692-0 Paperbound $2.50

THE MAGICAL MONARCH OF MO, L. Frank Baum. Remarkable adventures in a land even stranger than Oz. The best of Baum's books not in the Oz series. 15 color plates and dozens of drawings by Frank Verbeck. xviii + 237pp.
21892-9 Paperbound $2.00

THE BAD CHILD'S BOOK OF BEASTS, MORE BEASTS FOR WORSE CHILDREN, A MORAL ALPHABET, Hilaire Belloc. Three complete humor classics in one volume. Be kind to the frog, and do not call him names . . . and 28 other whimsical animals. Familiar favorites and some not so well known. Illustrated by Basil Blackwell. 156pp.
(USO) 20749-8 Paperbound $1.25

TWO LITTLE SAVAGES; BEING THE ADVENTURES OF TWO BOYS WHO LIVED AS INDIANS AND WHAT THEY LEARNED, Ernest Thompson Seton. Great classic of nature and boyhood provides a vast range of woodlore in most palatable form, a genuinely entertaining story. Two farm boys build a teepee in woods and live in it for a month, working out Indian solutions to living problems, star lore, birds and animals, plants, etc. 293 illustrations. vii + 286pp.

20985-7 Paperbound $2.50

PETER PIPER'S PRACTICAL PRINCIPLES OF PLAIN & PERFECT PRONUNCIATION. Alliterative jingles and tongue-twisters of surprising charm, that made their first appearance in America about 1830. Republished in full with the spirited woodcut illustrations from this earliest American edition. 32pp. $4\frac{1}{2}$ x $6\frac{3}{8}$.

22560-7 Paperbound $1.00

SCIENCE EXPERIMENTS AND AMUSEMENTS FOR CHILDREN, Charles Vivian. 73 easy experiments, requiring only materials found at home or easily available, such as candles, coins, steel wool, etc.; illustrate basic phenomena like vacuum, simple chemical reaction, etc. All safe. Modern, well-planned. Formerly *Science Games for Children*. 102 photos, numerous drawings. 96pp. $6\frac{1}{8}$ x $9\frac{1}{4}$.

21856-2 Paperbound $1.25

AN INTRODUCTION TO CHESS MOVES AND TACTICS SIMPLY EXPLAINED, Leonard Barden. Informal intermediate introduction, quite strong in explaining reasons for moves. Covers basic material, tactics, important openings, traps, positional play in middle game, end game. Attempts to isolate patterns and recurrent configurations. Formerly *Chess*. 58 figures. 102pp. (USO) 21210-6 Paperbound $1.25

LASKER'S MANUAL OF CHESS, Dr. Emanuel Lasker. Lasker was not only one of the five great World Champions, he was also one of the ablest expositors, theorists, and analysts. In many ways, his Manual, permeated with his philosophy of battle, filled with keen insights, is one of the greatest works ever written on chess. Filled with analyzed games by the great players. A single-volume library that will profit almost any chess player, beginner or master. 308 diagrams. xli x 349pp.

20640-8 Paperbound $2.75

THE MASTER BOOK OF MATHEMATICAL RECREATIONS, Fred Schuh. In opinion of many the finest work ever prepared on mathematical puzzles, stunts, recreations; exhaustively thorough explanations of mathematics involved, analysis of effects, citation of puzzles and games. Mathematics involved is elementary. Translated by F. Göbel. 194 figures. xxiv + 430pp.

22134-2 Paperbound $3.00

MATHEMATICS, MAGIC AND MYSTERY, Martin Gardner. Puzzle editor for Scientific American explains mathematics behind various mystifying tricks: card tricks, stage "mind reading," coin and match tricks, counting out games, geometric dissections, etc. Probability sets, theory of numbers clearly explained. Also provides more than 400 tricks, guaranteed to work, that you can do. 135 illustrations. xii + 176pp.

20338-2 Paperbound $1.50

How to Know the Wild Flowers, Mrs. William Starr Dana. This is the classical book of American wildflowers (of the Eastern and Central United States), used by hundreds of thousands. Covers over 500 species, arranged in extremely easy to use color and season groups. Full descriptions, much plant lore. This Dover edition is the fullest ever compiled, with tables of nomenclature changes. 174 full-page plates by M. Satterlee. xii + 418pp. 20332-8 Paperbound $2.75

Our Plant Friends and Foes, William Atherton DuPuy. History, economic importance, essential botanical information and peculiarities of 25 common forms of plant life are provided in this book in an entertaining and charming style. Covers food plants (potatoes, apples, beans, wheat, almonds, bananas, etc.), flowers (lily, tulip, etc.), trees (pine, oak, elm, etc.), weeds, poisonous mushrooms and vines, gourds, citrus fruits, cotton, the cactus family, and much more. 108 illustrations. xiv + 290pp. 22272-1 Paperbound $2.50

How to Know the Ferns, Frances T. Parsons. Classic survey of Eastern and Central ferns, arranged according to clear, simple identification key. Excellent introduction to greatly neglected nature area. 57 illustrations and 42 plates. xvi + 215pp. 20740-4 Paperbound $2.00

Manual of the Trees of North America, Charles S. Sargent. America's foremost dendrologist provides the definitive coverage of North American trees and tree-like shrubs. 717 species fully described and illustrated: exact distribution, down to township; full botanical description; economic importance; description of subspecies and races; habitat, growth data; similar material. Necessary to every serious student of tree-life. Nomenclature revised to present. Over 100 locating keys. 783 illustrations. lii + 934pp. 20277-1, 20278-X Two volumes, Paperbound $6.00

Our Northern Shrubs, Harriet L. Keeler. Fine non-technical reference work identifying more than 225 important shrubs of Eastern and Central United States and Canada. Full text covering botanical description, habitat, plant lore, is paralleled with 205 full-page photographs of flowering or fruiting plants. Nomenclature revised by Edward G. Voss. One of few works concerned with shrubs. 205 plates, 35 drawings. xxviii + 521pp. 21989-5 Paperbound $3.75

The Mushroom Handbook, Louis C. C. Krieger. Still the best popular handbook: full descriptions of 259 species, cross references to another 200. Extremely thorough text enables you to identify, know all about any mushroom you are likely to meet in eastern and central U. S. A.: habitat, luminescence, poisonous qualities, use, folklore, etc. 32 color plates show over 50 mushrooms, also 126 other illustrations. Finding keys. vii + 560pp. 21861-9 Paperbound $3.95

Handbook of Birds of Eastern North America, Frank M. Chapman. Still much the best single-volume guide to the birds of Eastern and Central United States. Very full coverage of 675 species, with descriptions, life habits, distribution, similar data. All descriptions keyed to two-page color chart. With this single volume the average birdwatcher needs no other books. 1931 revised edition. 195 illustrations. xxxvi + 581pp. 21489-3 Paperbound $4.50

THE PRINCIPLES OF PSYCHOLOGY, William James. The famous long course, complete and unabridged. Stream of thought, time perception, memory, experimental methods—these are only some of the concerns of a work that was years ahead of its time and still valid, interesting, useful. 94 figures. Total of xviii + 1391pp.
20381-6, 20382-4 Two volumes, Paperbound $8.00

THE STRANGE STORY OF THE QUANTUM, Banesh Hoffmann. Non-mathematical but thorough explanation of work of Planck, Einstein, Bohr, Pauli, de Broglie, Schrödinger, Heisenberg, Dirac, Feynman, etc. No technical background needed. "Of books attempting such an account, this is the best," Henry Margenau, Yale. 40-page "Postscript 1959." xii + 285pp. 20518-5 Paperbound $2.00

THE RISE OF THE NEW PHYSICS, A. d'Abro. Most thorough explanation in print of central core of mathematical physics, both classical and modern; from Newton to Dirac and Heisenberg. Both history and exposition; philosophy of science, causality, explanations of higher mathematics, analytical mechanics, electromagnetism, thermodynamics, phase rule, special and general relativity, matrices. No higher mathematics needed to follow exposition, though treatment is elementary to intermediate in level. Recommended to serious student who wishes verbal understanding. 97 illustrations. xvii + 982pp. 20003-5, 20004-3 Two volumes, Paperbound $6.00

GREAT IDEAS OF OPERATIONS RESEARCH, Jagjit Singh. Easily followed non-technical explanation of mathematical tools, aims, results: statistics, linear programming, game theory, queueing theory, Monte Carlo simulation, etc. Uses only elementary mathematics. Many case studies, several analyzed in detail. Clarity, breadth make this excellent for specialist in another field who wishes background. 41 figures. x + 228pp. 21886-1 Paperbound $2.50

GREAT IDEAS OF MODERN MATHEMATICS: THEIR NATURE AND USE, Jagjit Singh. Internationally famous expositor, winner of Unesco's Kalinga Award for science popularization explains verbally such topics as differential equations, matrices, groups, sets, transformations, mathematical logic and other important modern mathematics, as well as use in physics, astrophysics, and similar fields. Superb exposition for layman, scientist in other areas. viii + 312pp.
20587-8 Paperbound $2.50

GREAT IDEAS IN INFORMATION THEORY, LANGUAGE AND CYBERNETICS, Jagjit Singh. The analog and digital computers, how they work, how they are like and unlike the human brain, the men who developed them, their future applications, computer terminology. An essential book for today, even for readers with little math. Some mathematical demonstrations included for more advanced readers. 118 figures. Tables. ix + 338pp. 21694-2 Paperbound $2.50

CHANCE, LUCK AND STATISTICS, Horace C. Levinson. Non-mathematical presentation of fundamentals of probability theory and science of statistics and their applications. Games of chance, betting odds, misuse of statistics, normal and skew distributions, birth rates, stock speculation, insurance. Enlarged edition. Formerly "The Science of Chance." xiii + 357pp. 21007-3 Paperbound $2.50

PLANETS, STARS AND GALAXIES: DESCRIPTIVE ASTRONOMY FOR BEGINNERS, A. E. Fanning. Comprehensive introductory survey of astronomy: the sun, solar system, stars, galaxies, universe, cosmology; up-to-date, including quasars, radio stars, etc. Preface by Prof. Donald Menzel. 24pp. of photographs. 189pp. 5¼ x 8¼.
21680-2 Paperbound $1.50

TEACH YOURSELF CALCULUS, P. Abbott. With a good background in algebra and trig, you can teach yourself calculus with this book. Simple, straightforward introduction to functions of all kinds, integration, differentiation, series, etc. "Students who are beginning to study calculus method will derive great help from this book." Faraday House Journal. 308pp. 20683-1 Clothbound $2.00

TEACH YOURSELF TRIGONOMETRY, P. Abbott. Geometrical foundations, indices and logarithms, ratios, angles, circular measure, etc. are presented in this sound, easy-to-use text. Excellent for the beginner or as a brush up, this text carries the student through the solution of triangles. 204pp. 20682-3 Clothbound $2.00

TEACH YOURSELF ANATOMY, David LeVay. Accurate, inclusive, profusely illustrated account of structure, skeleton, abdomen, muscles, nervous system, glands, brain, reproductive organs, evolution. "Quite the best and most readable account,' Medical Officer. 12 color plates. 164 figures. 311pp. 4¾ x 7.
21651-9 Clothbound $2.50

TEACH YOURSELF PHYSIOLOGY, David LeVay. Anatomical, biochemical bases; digestive, nervous, endocrine systems; metabolism; respiration; muscle; excretion; temperature control; reproduction. "Good elementary exposition," The Lancet. 6 color plates. 44 illustrations. 208pp. 4¼ x 7. 21658-6 Clothbound $2.50

THE FRIENDLY STARS, Martha Evans Martin. Classic has taught naked-eye observation of stars, planets to hundreds of thousands, still not surpassed for charm, lucidity, adequacy. Completely updated by Professor Donald H. Menzel, Harvard Observatory. 25 illustrations. 16 x 30 chart. x + 147pp. 21099-5 Paperbound $1.25

MUSIC OF THE SPHERES: THE MATERIAL UNIVERSE FROM ATOM TO QUASAR, SIMPLY EXPLAINED, Guy Murchie. Extremely broad, brilliantly written popular account begins with the solar system and reaches to dividing line between matter and nonmatter; latest understandings presented with exceptional clarity. Volume One: Planets, stars, galaxies, cosmology, geology, celestial mechanics, latest astronomical discoveries; Volume Two: Matter, atoms, waves, radiation, relativity, chemical action, heat, nuclear energy, quantum theory, music, light, color, probability, antimatter, antigravity, and similar topics. 319 figures. 1967 (second) edition. Total of xx + 644pp. 21809-0, 21810-4 Two volumes, Paperbound $5.00

OLD-TIME SCHOOLS AND SCHOOL BOOKS, Clifton Johnson. Illustrations and rhymes from early primers, abundant quotations from early textbooks, many anecdotes of school life enliven this study of elementary schools from Puritans to middle 19th century. Introduction by Carl Withers. 234 illustrations. xxxiii + 381pp.
21031-6 Paperbound $2.50

THE PHILOSOPHY OF THE UPANISHADS, Paul Deussen. Clear, detailed statement of upanishadic system of thought, generally considered among best available. History of these works, full exposition of system emergent from them, parallel concepts in the West. Translated by A. S. Geden. xiv + 429pp.

21616-0 Paperbound $3.00

LANGUAGE, TRUTH AND LOGIC, Alfred J. Ayer. Famous, remarkably clear introduction to the Vienna and Cambridge schools of Logical Positivism; function of philosophy, elimination of metaphysical thought, nature of analysis, similar topics. "Wish I had written it myself," Bertrand Russell. 2nd, 1946 edition. 160pp.

20010-8 Paperbound $1.35

THE GUIDE FOR THE PERPLEXED, Moses Maimonides. Great classic of medieval Judaism, major attempt to reconcile revealed religion (Pentateuch, commentaries) and Aristotelian philosophy. Enormously important in all Western thought. Unabridged Friedländer translation. 50-page introduction. lix + 414pp.

(USO) 20351-4 Paperbound $2.50

OCCULT AND SUPERNATURAL PHENOMENA, D. H. Rawcliffe. Full, serious study of the most persistent delusions of mankind: crystal gazing, mediumistic trance, stigmata, lycanthropy, fire walking, dowsing, telepathy, ghosts, ESP, etc., and their relation to common forms of abnormal psychology. Formerly *Illusions and Delusions of the Supernatural and the Occult.* iii + 551pp. 20503-7 Paperbound $3.50

THE EGYPTIAN BOOK OF THE DEAD: THE PAPYRUS OF ANI, E. A. Wallis Budge. Full hieroglyphic text, interlinear transliteration of sounds, word for word translation, then smooth, connected translation; Theban recension. Basic work in Ancient Egyptian civilization; now even more significant than ever for historical importance, dilation of consciousness, etc. clvi + 377pp. 6½ x 9¼.

21866-X Paperbound $3.95

PSYCHOLOGY OF MUSIC, Carl E. Seashore. Basic, thorough survey of everything known about psychology of music up to 1940's; essential reading for psychologists, musicologists. Physical acoustics; auditory apparatus; relationship of physical sound to perceived sound; role of the mind in sorting, altering, suppressing, creating sound sensations; musical learning, testing for ability, absolute pitch, other topics. Records of Caruso, Menuhin analyzed. 88 figures. xix + 408pp.

21851-1 Paperbound $2.75

THE I CHING (THE BOOK OF CHANGES), translated by James Legge. Complete translated text plus appendices by Confucius, of perhaps the most penetrating divination book ever compiled. Indispensable to all study of early Oriental civilizations. 3 plates. xxiii + 448pp. 21062-6 Paperbound $3.00

THE UPANISHADS, translated by Max Müller. Twelve classical upanishads: Chandogya, Kena, Aitareya, Kaushitaki, Isa, Katha, Mundaka, Taittiriyaka, Brhadaranyaka, Svetasvatara, Prasna, Maitriyana. 160-page introduction, analysis by Prof. Müller. Total of 826pp. 20398-0, 20399-9 Two volumes, Paperbound $5.00

INCIDENTS OF TRAVEL IN YUCATAN, John L. Stephens. Classic (1843) exploration of jungles of Yucatan, looking for evidences of Maya civilization. Stephens found many ruins; comments on travel adventures, Mexican and Indian culture. 127 striking illustrations by F. Catherwood. Total of 669 pp.
20926-1, 20927-X Two volumes, Paperbound $5.00

INCIDENTS OF TRAVEL IN CENTRAL AMERICA, CHIAPAS, AND YUCATAN, John L. Stephens. An exciting travel journal and an important classic of archeology. Narrative relates his almost single-handed discovery of the Mayan culture, and exploration of the ruined cities of Copan, Palenque, Utatlan and others; the monuments they dug from the earth, the temples buried in the jungle, the customs of poverty-stricken Indians living a stone's throw from the ruined palaces. 115 drawings by F. Catherwood. Portrait of Stephens. xii + 812pp.
22404-X, 22405-8 Two volumes, Paperbound $6.00

A NEW VOYAGE ROUND THE WORLD, William Dampier. Late 17-century naturalist joined the pirates of the Spanish Main to gather information; remarkably vivid account of buccaneers, pirates; detailed, accurate account of botany, zoology, ethnography of lands visited. Probably the most important early English voyage, enormous implications for British exploration, trade, colonial policy. Also most interesting reading. Argonaut edition, introduction by Sir Albert Gray. New introduction by Percy Adams. 6 plates, 7 illustrations. xlvii + 376pp. 6½ x 9¼.
21900-3 Paperbound $3.00

INTERNATIONAL AIRLINE PHRASE BOOK IN SIX LANGUAGES, Joseph W. Bátor. Important phrases and sentences in English paralleled with French, German, Portuguese, Italian, Spanish equivalents, covering all possible airport-travel situations; created for airline personnel as well as tourist by Language Chief, Pan American Airlines. xiv + 204pp.
22017-6 Paperbound $2.00

STAGE COACH AND TAVERN DAYS, Alice Morse Earle. Detailed, lively account of the early days of taverns; their uses and importance in the social, political and military life; furnishings and decorations; locations; food and drink; tavern signs, etc. Second half covers every aspect of early travel; the roads, coaches, drivers, etc. Nostalgic, charming, packed with fascinating material. 157 illustrations, mostly photographs. xiv + 449pp.
22518-6 Paperbound $4.00

NORSE DISCOVERIES AND EXPLORATIONS IN NORTH AMERICA, Hjalmar R. Holand. The perplexing Kensington Stone, found in Minnesota at the end of the 19th century. Is it a record of a Scandinavian expedition to North America in the 14th century? Or is it one of the most successful hoaxes in history. A scientific detective investigation. Formerly *Westward from Vinland*. 31 photographs, 17 figures. x + 354pp.
22014-1 Paperbound $2.75

A BOOK OF OLD MAPS, compiled and edited by Emerson D. Fite and Archibald Freeman. 74 old maps offer an unusual survey of the discovery, settlement and growth of America down to the close of the Revolutionary war: maps showing Norse settlements in Greenland, the explorations of Columbus, Verrazano, Cabot, Champlain, Joliet, Drake, Hudson, etc., campaigns of Revolutionary war battles, and much more. Each map is accompanied by a brief historical essay. xvi + 299pp. 11 x 13¾.
22084-2 Paperbound $6.00

MATHEMATICAL PUZZLES FOR BEGINNERS AND ENTHUSIASTS, Geoffrey Mott-Smith. 189 puzzles from easy to difficult—involving arithmetic, logic, algebra, properties of digits, probability, etc.—for enjoyment and mental stimulus. Explanation of mathematical principles behind the puzzles. 135 illustrations. viii + 248pp.
20198-8 Paperbound $1.75

PAPER FOLDING FOR BEGINNERS, William D. Murray and Francis J. Rigney. Easiest book on the market, clearest instructions on making interesting, beautiful origami. Sail boats, cups, roosters, frogs that move legs, bonbon boxes, standing birds, etc. 40 projects; more than 275 diagrams and photographs. 94pp.
20713-7 Paperbound $1.00

TRICKS AND GAMES ON THE POOL TABLE, Fred Herrmann. 79 tricks and games— some solitaires, some for two or more players, some competitive games—to entertain you between formal games. Mystifying shots and throws, unusual caroms, tricks involving such props as cork, coins, a hat, etc. Formerly *Fun on the Pool Table*. 77 figures. 95pp.
21814-7 Paperbound $1.00

HAND SHADOWS TO BE THROWN UPON THE WALL: A SERIES OF NOVEL AND AMUSING FIGURES FORMED BY THE HAND, Henry Bursill. Delightful picturebook from great-grandfather's day shows how to make 18 different hand shadows: a bird that flies, duck that quacks, dog that wags his tail, camel, goose, deer, boy, turtle, etc. Only book of its sort. vi + 33pp. 6½ x 9¼. 21779-5 Paperbound $1.00

WHITTLING AND WOODCARVING, E. J. Tangerman. 18th printing of best book on market. "If you can cut a potato you can carve" toys and puzzles, chains, chessmen, caricatures, masks, frames, woodcut blocks, surface patterns, much more. Information on tools, woods, techniques. Also goes into serious wood sculpture from Middle Ages to present, East and West. 464 photos, figures. x + 293pp.
20965-2 Paperbound $2.00

HISTORY OF PHILOSOPHY, Julián Marias. Possibly the clearest, most easily followed, best planned, most useful one-volume history of philosophy on the market, neither skimpy nor overfull. Full details on system of every major philosopher and dozens of less important thinkers from pre-Socratics up to Existentialism and later. Strong on many European figures usually omitted. Has gone through dozens of editions in Europe. 1966 edition, translated by Stanley Appelbaum and Clarence Strowbridge. xviii + 505pp.
21739-6 Paperbound $3.00

YOGA: A SCIENTIFIC EVALUATION, Kovoor T. Behanan. Scientific but non-technical study of physiological results of yoga exercises; done under auspices of Yale U. Relations to Indian thought, to psychoanalysis, etc. 16 photos. xxiii + 270pp.
20505-3 Paperbound $2.50

Prices subject to change without notice.
Available at your book dealer or write for free catalogue to Dept. GI, Dover Publications, Inc., 180 Varick St., N. Y., N. Y. 10014. Dover publishes more than 150 books each year on science, elementary and advanced mathematics, biology, music, art, literary history, social sciences and other areas.